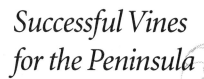

Successful Vines
for the Peninsula

a selection
by members of
Western Horticultural Society

edited by Elaine Levine
illustrated by Mabel Crittenden and Nancy Carman Schramm
design by Carol Moholt

published by Western Horticultural Society
Palo Alto, California

Western Horticultural Society

Printed in the United States of America
Published 1996

Library of Congress Catalog Card Number 96–060292
ISBN 0-9622226-1-5

First Printing 1996

Western
Horticultural Society
P. O. Box 60507
Palo Alto, CA 94306

Dedicated to
Albert Wilson
1902 - 1996

At the age of four he survived the 1906 earthquake in an orphanage on the sand dunes at the western end of San Francisco. A graduate of Lowell High School, he worked his way through Stanford University with a degree in botany. He taught at San Mateo College for 28 years. His radio program was on the air for some 40 years and his "Dig It With Albert" television program almost as long. "How Does Your Garden Grow?" was his first book. "These Were the Children" told of his life in the orphanage. He appeared at hundreds of garden shows and spoke at thousands of garden clubs. A charter member of Western Horticulture Society, he enlivened many meetings. With his beret trademark, he became a legend in his lifetime.

Contents

Introduction

"Successful Vines for the Peninsula" is a companion book to "Successful Perennials for the Peninsula."

Like the perennials book, this book on vines is written by members of the Western Horticultural Society who have grown or are growing the plant described under conditions encountered by most home gardeners. Members of the society are both professional and amateur gardeners (the latter usually accurately depicted as avid). We want to share our knowledge and enthusiasm with the beginning gardener or one new to the Peninsula. The list of contributors appears in the back.

Vines, for the purposes of this book, are climbing plants that need support. Some, like plumbago, are shrubby and are able to grow (or sprawl) on their own; others, such as ivy, without support, will become ground covers.

Each writer has described the plant, flower color (if any), and growing conditions. Sources, especially for those not easily found at retail nurseries, are usually listed. We encourage readers to ask their local nurseries for deserving plants to try to broaden the diversity that is available on the Peninsula.

Vines, because of their tendency to become tangled, are not favorites of garden centers, and are ordinarily found at the rear of the nursery. Although they often are not attractive in the nursery pot, vines serve a useful function in the landscape, particularly for those with small spaces. No room for a tree to screen an ugly view? A vine can occupy a couple of feet of ground. An unattractive fence? A neglected area with no water? A tree or shrub that looks dull most of the year? A vine could fill the bill.

We have provided at the back of the book lists of characteristics such as flower color, sun and water requirements, and rate of growth to help the reader chose the appropriate vine. We hope there will be at least one vine here that will meet your needs and expectations.

The vines in this book, as in most plant encyclopedias, are listed alphabetically by botanical name. While some of the botanical names are tongue-twisters, using common names leads to confusion. A trumpet vine, for example, can be any number of different vines. A morning glory can be a perennial or an annual. There is a cross reference at the back of the book to help you find the plant you want.

As for pronunciation, Dick Dunmire contributes a droll verse on the subject using clematis as an example:

"Some folks will be real mad at us
If we call the vine, clem-AT-is.
Others, though, will haw and hem at us
If we pronounce it CLEM-atis.
And they surely would berate us
If we pronounce it clem-ATE-us."

There are a couple of categories of climbing plants we have not included. Except for the Lady Banks rose, there are no climbing roses. They require a book by themselves.

Unless a vine with edible fruit has ornamental value, we have not included it either. We have kiwi, but not grapes. Scarlet runner beans are included for their flowers.

Descriptions have been checked against authorities such as *Hortus III* and the Royal Horticultural Society's *Index to Garden Plants* and the Royal Horticultural Society's *Dictionary of Gardening*.

We are indebted to Dr. Elizabeth McClintock, Research Associate, The Herbarium, University of California, Berkeley, for her considerable help on botanical questions. Elizabeth Garbett, Dick Dunmire and Ed Carman spent many hours on fact-checking. Carol Moholt was production manager. Nancy McClenny, Rosamond Bray, Ruth Lacey, Marjorie Branagh, and Mabel Crittenden were also on the book committee.

We are also grateful to Mabel Crittenden and Nancy Carman Schramm for the illustrations.

For more information about these vines or other plants, the reader is invited to join the Western Horticultural Society, P.O. Box 60507, Palo Alto, CA 94306. Meeting date is the second Wednesday of the month, and visitors are welcome.

Elaine Levine

ABUTILON MEGAPOTAMICUM
Malvaceae
FLOWERING MAPLE
Evergreen perennial

Abutilon is a heat-loving shrubby vine with leaves that resemble the maple from which it gets its common name, flowering maple.

In an eastern or southern exposure, preferably under an overhang for frost protection, it will flower nearly year–round, its small red or yellow bells providing hummingbird food at a time when other nectar sources are scarce.

Flowering maple grows rapidly to 10 or 12 feet, but needs tying to a trellis for support. If it should get frost-bitten, it will come back from the roots.

BB

ACTINIDIA DELICIOSA (ACTINIDIA CHINENSIS)
Actinidiaceae
KIWI VINE, CHINESE GOOSEBERRY, YANGTAO
Deciduous perennial

Kiwi is a deciduous, strong growing, twining vine that can grow to 50 feet or more in length. It is native to the forest understory in the Yangtze Valley and other areas of China. Seeds were taken to New Zealand about 1900 where plants were propagated and started the kiwi industry in that country. Many selections of fruit types have been made in New Zealand, the best of which were first shipped to California in the early 1970's. About that same time growers in California began importing plants to start commercial production of kiwi fruit here.

These dioecious vines (male and female are separate plants) produce a hairy, brown-skinned fruit that has bright green flesh enclosing tiny black seeds. Botanically the kiwi fruit is a berry. The fruit size varies with the cultivated variety, from the long narrow 'Bruno', about 2 ounces to the almost round 'Hayward' or 'Chico', about 4 ounces. 'Hayward' or 'Chico' cultivars are available in the markets. They are probably the same fruit with different names, as they are identical as far as anyone can tell.

The plants bloom in May and June, bees pollinate the two–inch single creamy white flowers, and the fruit is ready to pick in the fall. Commercial growers pick when the sugar level is just over 7%, which is usually October in the Central Valley, and late November in the coastal areas.

The fruit is hard at this time and can be stored in plastic bags in the refrigerator for six months or more. It will help keep fruit from spoil-ing in storage if the hairs and blossom end are cleaned with a stiff brush. To ripen, kiwi fruit are placed in a plastic bag on the counter with an apple until just soft to the touch when they are ready to eat. With green flesh, shiny black seeds, and a white core, the fruit is very decorative in fruit sal-ads and as a garnish on other dishes. Cut in half they can be spooned out of the skin and eaten. They make an excellent marmalade when cooked with a small amount of orange. When dried, kiwi is a tart snack.

Kiwi fruit

Kiwi vines have a fibrous, spreading root system so they should be planted in a light, well–drained soil. If grown in heavy soils they should be elevated on a slight mound so that water will not stand around the crown of the roots in the winter. Young plants will need extra water-ing, and established vines will probably need water at least once a week all summer. Any wilting or leaf burn generally indicates lack of water. A good mulch will help conserve water and a 3 to 4–foot space around the base of the plant should be kept free of any other growth. A high nitro-gen fertilizer is used during the summer growing season.

These large, strong growing vines must be trained on a sturdy support. A simple structure can be made with 2–inch by 4–inch posts spaced about 10 feet apart. Holes are drilled 7 feet above the ground so that a 8 gauge wire may be strung, tensioned, and well braced to hold the weight of the vine and fruit.

The vines are planted between the posts with a small stake to guide the leader to the horizontal support. The leader is pinched at the wire so that it will branch. These shoots can then be trained along the wire to make the permanent cordon or framework of the vine. While training a new vine all growth must be tied and not allowed to twine around any of the supports. As the cordon is trained along the horizontal supports, side laterals will develop which will be the fruit spurs. These spurs will grow out from the main cordon from 5 to 20 feet each year. The trellis should be about 25 feet long with the female plant trained along 20 feet while the male can be kept to 5 feet, adequate to produce flowers to pollinate the female.

Kiwi male (left) and female flowers

Kiwi flowers are used to identify the sex of the plant. Female flowers have a small immature fruit at the base of the petals with a white irregular stigma surrounded by yellow anthers. The male flower has only yellow anthers loaded with pollen. Generally there will be up to 6 flowers on a single stem on the male plant while the female has only 1 to 3 flowers at a node. All flowers usually have 6 petals. A female plant with 25 feet of cordon could produce up to 100 pounds of fruit five years after planting.

Kiwis make an excellent arbor cover providing the arbor is at least 25 feet by 10 feet The vines must be pruned just as soon as all the leaves have fallen, generally January or early February. If pruned in March or later there is danger of excessive bleeding as the sap starts to flow long before the new growth shows. Young plants that have not fruited will have little to prune except for some laterals which are cut back to within eight inches of the main cordon. Any sucker growth from the ground should be removed. As plants mature and begin fruiting the spurs are cut, leaving two buds of current growth beyond the fruit stems which are left when picking the fruit. Because the fruit spur becomes longer each year it will be necessary after five or six years to cut this spur back to the cordon and start another spur.

Summer growth may be cut back so long as about 4 feet is maintained beyond the fruit to protect it from sunburn. Snails may do extensive damage to new growth of young plants. No other pests are a problem for the home gardener.

Kiwi can be grown from seed but it may take 5 to 10 years to fruit and then could be worthless. Propagation is by soft or hardwood cuttings in most cases. Kiwi is easy to graft while dormant. If seedlings are used as understock they should be pencil size, with scions the same diameter, using a side graft for the best results. If grafting canes over one inch in diameter the cleft graft works best with a smaller scion at each edge of the stock. Grafting is done in late January and all cut edges sealed. As with any other fruiting plant you must be sure of the cutting source and keep scions labeled as they can only be identified when in bloom. With care the kiwi vine can produce for more than forty years.

EC

AKEBIA QUINATA
Lardizabalaceae
FIVE-LEAF AKEBIA
Evergreen perennial

The five-leaved akebia is an excellent vine for producing a delicate tracery against a wall or for use as a screen.

The foliage of *Akebia quinata* is its chief beauty. The dark green leaves are palmately compound, the five, small notched leaflets radiating fan-wise from their point of attachment on the petiole. They are well presented, standing away from the vine on long petioles. The slender, twining stems can reach 15 feet and are fast–growing, so, despite its dainty appearance, this vine needs a firm hand to keep it under control. It is tolerant of pruning at any time.

Elizabeth Garbett's akebia grows beside a walkway and is constantly reaching out exploratory tendrils that need to be dealt with from time to time. It can be cut to the ground if necessary and will quickly resprout.

The dark purple flowers are more curious than beautiful. Male and female flowers are separate but borne in the same cluster; the female flowers are a dull purple with three cupped petals and a cluster of pistils while the male flowers are smaller, more numerous and somewhat brighter purple. The fruits, when produced, are three–inch ovoid berries, purple with black seeds. They are edible, but not very palatable, being bland and sweetish.

Except for very cold winters, it is evergreen and hardy to cold. Akebia will tolerate almost any exposure from sun to part shade. Always presentable, nearly pest-free, it is one of the handsomest of small–leaved vines. The form *A. quinata* 'Variegata' has creamy white variegation on the leaves and is best grown in part shade. It has fragrant reddish–purple flowers.

EG, SA, MG

AMPELOPSIS
Vitaceae
BLUEBERRY VINE
Deciduous perennial

Members of the genus *Ampelopsis*, deciduous climbers in the grape family, are not widely cultivated, although they are hardy, have elegant foliage, and (often) display attractive fruit. The plant Dick Dunmire is familiar with is probably *A. aconitifolia,* although it nearly matches the description of *A. brevipedunculata* 'Citrulloides'. *A. aconitifolia* has berries that pass from green to yellow, then blue and finally brown or orange while berries of *A. brevipedunculata* are bright blue or purplish.

Its slender, quick-growing stems are well clothed with 5–inch deep green leaves that are cut deeply into 5 lobes, with each lobe deeply toothed or cut. Opposite each leaf is a branched tendril bearing sucking disks which cling to wood, bark, or masonry. Small clusters of inconspicuous green flowers are followed by peppercorn–sized fruits. Dick Dunmire's plant, lacking solid support, weaves through a wire fence, occasionally throwing out a stem to invade a nearby dwarf apple or trail along the ground. Although vigorous, it is not invasive and is easy to control with a few snips of the pruning shears. Beyond the fence it covers a 10-foot by 3-foot patch of baked clay between fence and road as a ground cover. A native of northern China and Mongolia, it is hardy to any cold experienced here, and his specimen survives on a very small ration of water. It grows in hottest sun, but is reputed to thrive in shade as well.

  Ampelopsis brevipedunculata 'Elegans' is truly a fitting name for this elegant vine. The 3-inch green, gray and white variegated leaves are palmate with 3 to 5 lobes. The new growth is white flushed pink as it first emerges, gradually turning to the mature variegation. As the new growth elongates new pink leaves appear at each node toward the crown of the plant. The overall effect is light and airy with the new pink foliage scattered throughout the plant. The stems are a rosy red, as are the tendrils that hold this *Ampelopsis* in place as it can even climb a window screen. This vine makes an excellent hanging basket which should be kept in partial shade to obtain the best leaf color. Fruits that set in the late summer are a beautiful porcelain blue. Propagation is by cuttings or seed. Regular pruning in the spring before growth starts will develop a full basket of the attractive foliage. Native to Japan and Korea, this vine will make an outstanding bonsai.

EC, DD

ARISTOLOCHIA CALIFORNICA
Aristolochiaceae
CALIFORNIA DUTCHMAN'S PIPE, PIPEVINE
Deciduous perennial

  California pipevine, *Aristolochia californica,* is an oddity similar to the eastern native Dutchman's pipe, *A. macrophylla,* but more suited to our climate because it is a California native. *A. macrophylla* doesn't like our mild winters, and further, its distinctive flowers are hidden by its leaves.

A. californica can be found on rocky slopes of the Sierra foothills twined in shrubs and trees which provide the light shade it needs.

In the garden, it can be grown against a fence, on a pergola with morning sun, or, as in nature, scrambling up a tree.

In late winter, the bare stems sport odd little meerschaum pipes of greenish-purple flowers before the heart-shaped leaves come out. At a time of year when little else is blooming, it will be exclaimed upon by every garden visitor.

California Native Plant Society growers recommend that it not be watered after August to allow it to go dormant to mimic its native habitat. But the experience of others indicates it tolerates water year–round.

Pipevine can grow several feet in a season to 12 feet. It requires no fertilizing and moderate water. Since it grows by twining, provide something on which it can climb. Cup hooks attached to a fence is one idea.

Another plus for the plant is as a food source for the larvae of the pipevine swallowtail butterfly.

Propagation is by rooted divisions easily dug up when it puts on new growth in the spring. It can also be purchased at nurseries specializing in native plants or at native plant sales.

CC, SA, EL

ASARINA SCANDENS
Scrophulariaceae
CREEPING GLOXINIA
Evergreen perennial

Asarina scandens, creeping gloxinia, is native to Mexico. Densely pubescent, the stems and leaves feel as if they are made of felt. The dark green, 3–inch, deltoid leaves are coarsely notched. The leaf petiole clasps any twig or branch to support the vine as it clambers through shrubbery.

Asarina scandens

The 3-inch, lavender-pink, gloxinia-like flowers are produced toward the tips of the new growth. With training, it would make a basket plant for a sunny patio. By using a wire frame or three branches of bamboo or birch to make a tepee structure, a free-standing cone could be developed.

Easily grown from seed (one source is Thompson and Morgan), it will bloom the first season if started early. If protected from freezing, it will bloom through December. Non-flowering tip cuttings can be rooted. A white form is listed by the Royal Horticultural Society. Thompson and Morgan's Jewel Mix comes in white, pink and blue-violet.

EC

ASPARAGUS
Liliaceae
SICKLE THORN ASPARAGUS
Evergreen perennial

The sickle–thorn asparagus, *A. falcatus,* is the most commanding vine of its genus, which includes several more fine–textured climbers (including one attractive pest), some shrubby or sub–shrubby plants, and, of course, the asparagus we eat. All are characterized by the absence of true leaves, the food–manufacturing chores being assumed by leaflike branchlets called cladodes. All have minute white or whitish flowers followed by small red to brown or black berries. They are among the few climbers in the lily family (Liliaceae).

A. falcatus climbs by twining and by using its curved thorns; in our gardens it is usually seen as a 20–foot plant, but it can grow taller. Narrow dark green cladodes are the largest in the genus, reaching 3 inches in length, giving the plant the aspect of a climbing *Podocarpus macrophyllus*. Naked shoots emerge from the roots and rapidly climb to their full height before producing foliage. Tiny clustered flowers are mildly fragrant. Stems last for several years, but the oldest should be pruned out to avoid a hopeless, thorny tangle; wear stout gloves when pruning.

Plants are greenest and least liable to frost damage in partial to full shade, although they tolerate sun near the coast. Roots survive even hard frost, and regrowth is rapid. Plants like average garden water, but can withstand short periods of drought. Use it to cover a post, wall, or trellis.

A. setaceus, more widely sold as *A. plumosus*, the fern asparagus, has tiny cladodes in flat, fernlike sprays which are often used in place of fern in floral arrangements. It can grow from 10 to 20 feet tall, and occasionally volunteers from bird–sown seeds.

A. asparagoides, smilax, is a twiner with inch–long, sharp–pointed, bright glossy green cladodes on twining stems that arise from a clump of fleshy roots. It can reach 20 feet, but in unwatered gardens is much smaller. Although foliage is attractive in bouquets and wreaths or on a wall or trellis, smilax can become a pest from volunteer seeding. Plants can survive any drought, simply drying up until rain comes, when they sprout rapidly from the immortal, tuberous roots.

    A. crispus and *A. scandens* are rarely seen delicate climbers usually grown (if grown at all) in hanging baskets. Delicate cladodes grow on zig–zag drooping branches.

DD

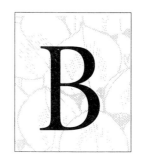

BILLARDIERA LONGIFLORA
Pittosporaceae
Evergreen perennial

Native to Tasmania, *Billardiera longiflora* is an evergreen, wiry vine with dark green, lanceolate leaves carried on thin black stems. The pendulous, pale yellow to chartreuse flowers are just over an inch long, tubular with a bell shaped opening. These make a good show in March and April; as they fade to purple, there appear to be yellow and purple flowers at the same time.

Billardiera forms a fleshy fruit less than an inch long and filled with small seeds, usually purple in color. There are pink and white forms, which must be grown from cuttings. The fruit stays on the vine well into the fall gradually drying to a brown.

This vine can be grown from seed or softwood cuttings. Plants are available from Western Hills Rare Plant Nursery, Occidental, or Carman's Nursery, Los Gatos.

It can be easily be kept to a 6 or 8–foot trellis. It requires good drainage, regular water and should be grown in shade. Our plant survived the 1990 freeze of 16 degrees.

Billardiera makes an excellent pot plant that can be trained to a standard or a column on a wire frame. As a pot plant it can be displayed on the patio or deck while in flower and fruit, and replaced with another flowering pot during the winter. It is seldom bothered by any pests.

EC

Billardiera flowering stem

BOUGAINVILLEA
Nyctaginaceae
Evergreen perennial

For blazing color over a long period, few plants can match *Bougainvillea glabra (B. brasiliensis)*. Although its tropical origin makes it susceptible to frost on the Peninsula, two steps can be taken to make its success more likely, if not to ensure it—plant bougainvillea in a sunny, sheltered corner and put in new plants in early spring to allow roots to become established before winter frost.

Bougainvillea has a fine, delicate root system that is easily injured during the transplanting process. To avoid tearing the almost-microscopic size root ends, cut off the bottom of the container, slit its sides and carefully move the soil ball into the ground.

Bougainvillea is fast–growing, covering a wall or sturdy trellis with thorny, stiff stems that can be kept in control by pruning. Leaves are ovate and entire. It is evergreen.

Color in bougainvillea is not in the inconspicuous yellowish-white flower, but in the bracts surrounding them. The familiar purple and red cultivars are among the easiest to grow and most vigorous— Look for 'San Diego Red' and 'Barbara Karst' if you want a vibrantly-colored, easy to grow, bougainvillea.

Softer shades are also available, ranging from white through pale pink or yellow to burnt orange. If you choose a bougainvillea from among the paler–colored cultivars, make sure you plant it in the warmest, most sheltered location possible. Faithfully water and fertilize the first few seasons to help it get established here on the peninsula.

Once established bougainvillea requires little water. Should it freeze, another can be grown quickly. When pruning or removing, wear protective clothing against its thorns.

EL, CM

CALYSTEGIA MACROSTEGIA
Convolvulaceae
WILD MORNING GLORY
Deciduous perennial

A good choice for the native garden, the wild morning glory is well adapted to our climate, although *Calystegia macrostegia* originates in the Channel Islands, *C. occidentalis* is native to northern California. Neither is easy to find, but it is worth looking for in native plant sales or at native plant nurseries. (I found mine at Yerba Buena.)

C. macrostegia 'Anacapa Pink' blooms a whitish–pink (or a pinkish–white) with typical morning glory blossoms in a big spring display, and with a little water, more modestly all summer.

When fall comes and it loses its leaves, it should be cut to the ground. In spring it sends out new shoots and is in bloom shortly thereafter, clambering up a fence or into bushes and trees.

Use them as you would cultivated morning glories. Like most natives, it needs water to get established; then little summer water is required.

EL

CANARINA CANARIENSIS
Campanulaceae
CANARY BELLFLOWER
Deciduous perennial

Canarina canariensis is a seldom seen member of Campanulaceae that is native to the woodlands of the Canary Islands. It has tubers, fleshy stems and foliage, and goes completely dormant for about six months of the year. Growth starts in December or January as the succulent leaves emerge from a pot that has had little or no water for up to three months. It is happy to scramble up other shrubs to about 6 feet where the 2-inch orange–yellow, waxy flowers are produced at the tips of the plant. The bell shaped flowers have dark maroon veins and the 1-inch fruit is supposed to be edible but consists mainly of seeds and a little mucilage.

Canarina must have a humus–rich soil and good drainage and be placed in filtered sun. After flowering the foliage will gradually turn brown and water should be slowly withheld and stopped when the growth has dried. In containers they need not be watered until growth starts in the fall. When planted in the garden they would not survive a heavy freeze and container plants should be kept just above freezing. It is a special plant to be displayed while in bloom and removed to a growing area when at rest.

EC

CELASTRUS SCANDENS
Celastraceae
BITTERSWEET
Deciduous perennial

Bittersweet, *Celastrus scandens,* is grown for its clustered showy orange berries which appear before the foliage falls in autumn. The 3-valved fruits open to display seeds enclosed in red arils. They remain on the plant for some time. In their native Eastern U.S. habitat, the berries are a favorite holiday decoration.

The flowers are small, greenish–yellow and inconspicuous. The leaves resemble those of a lilac and turn a golden yellow in fall.

It takes regular water, no fertilizer and likes protection from broiling afternoon sun.

My 30-year-old bittersweet has climbed 20 feet into and through a crabapple. When it didn't bear fruit, I learned it required a male and a female, and I had only a female. A male plant produced the desired result.

It can be propagated from seed or semi-ripe cuttings. I sent for mine from an Eastern source.

BW

CISSUS STRIATA
Vitaceae
Evergreen perennial

Cissus striata is the perfect vine for that ugly chain link fence or other fence or wall that needs a pleasing cover. From Chile, this member of Vitaceae climbs with very fine tendrils. The new growth of the angular stems is reddish. Glossy, dark green 5–parted leaves, somewhat toothed, are 1 to 3 inches across.

The tiny, decorative, bright red buds produce minute flowers that develop into clusters of small blue-purple fruits about the size of currants which may be enjoyed by the birds in summer.

A little slow to get started, but with regular water, *Cissus striata* can grow 6 to 8 feet a year. To make a thick cover, pinch the new tips frequently to encourage branching. If mature plantings become over-grown, they can be clipped back almost to the main stems. This should be done in the spring so the new growth will quickly grow out for a fresh, new look.

Cissus striata is a hardy evergreen vine that will grow in sun and part shade, is practically pest free, and looks good the year round.

EC

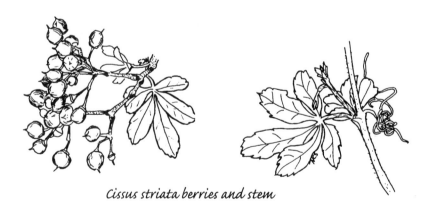

Cissus striata berries and stem

CLEMATIS
Ranunculaceae
Deciduous perennial

There are more than 300 species of clematis native to one or another of the temperate regions of the globe. They are, for the most part, deciduous, climbing or sprawling vines that attach themselves to their support by twining petioles.

There is great variety in the form of the flowers; they may be bell, urn, or saucer-shaped. The flower consists of colored sepals (no petals), many stamens, and a cluster or spiral of pistils that, when fertilized, develop into seeds, each with a long, feathery tail. These pinwheel–like seedheads are nearly as attractive as the flowers and are greatly prized by flower arrangers.

Only a fraction of clematis species are of garden value and most of these have relatively small, though charming flowers, often borne in great profusion. But to most people, clematis means the gorgeously–colored, large–flowered hybrids. These hybrids are of relatively recent origin. The first ones were created in the mid–1800's when a large–flowered species discovered in China was crossed with a Japanese species. Additional crosses were made with *C. viticella* from southern Europe and *C. florida,* another Chinese species. The results of these crosses generated great excitement among nurserymen, especially in England, and literally hundreds of named hybrids appeared in the trade. Today the range of colors, forms and sizes is vast and the popularity of clematis seems to grow every year.

The cultural requirements of clematis are essentially the same for the species and the hybrids. The soil should be light, well-drained and rich in organic matter, but not acidic. Clematis need to have their roots cool and shaded, but their heads in the sun. Covering the area around the roots with mulch or stones will help keep the roots cool.

Regular watering and feeding is a must for good performance. The species clematis are, as a rule, tougher and more vigorous than the hybrids, whose tenuous hold on life is exemplified by the brittle and almost invisible wire-thin stems connecting the

Clematis cirhossa seed

vine to the ground. Some gardeners surround the stem with a wire cage to protect it, especially from themselves, for there is no more bitter moment in a gardener's life than finding that, in an orgy of weeding, you have snapped the stem of your clematis by mistake.

Clematis cirrhosa

Clematis need a support of some kind. Usually grown on fences or trellises, they can be trained to sprawl over shrubs or climb into a tree. They combine well with climbing roses, their delicate stems twining easily through the sturdier rose canes. The large–flowered hybrid clematis are slow to get started and need several years to come into their full glory. When the root system is well developed, however, they start up with a rush in the spring and scramble up to the top of the trellis with amazing speed.

There are clematis that will bloom in almost any month of the year if you are willing to seek out some of the more exotic species. *C. cirrhosa* and *C. napaulensis* are both winter-blooming. *C. cirrhosa* has four greenish–white, bell-shaped sepals and can bloom in December or January in our area. *C. napaulensis* is similar but is summer–dormant. These are quiet, undramatic plants, but this a time when any bloom is welcome.

They are followed in February and March by the evergreen species *C. armandii* whose panicles of white flowers are dramatic against the dark foliage and are deliciously fragrant. There is a pink version, *C. armandii* 'Hendersonii Rubra', a very pale pink, not scented but appealing nevertheless. *C. armandii* is a very vigorous vine and needs to be pruned after flowering to keep it in check.

April is a wonderful month for clematis. At the beginning of the month there are many versions of the montana group with flowers from white (vanilla–scented) to shades of pink and rose. *C. montana* is a vigorous vine that can swallow a small building or a big fence in a short time. It is a most prodigous bloomer, the 2–inch, 4–sepalled flowers covering the vine in its once–a–year extravaganza. If necessary, pruning should be done just after flowering because the vine needs to produce wood this season for next season's flowers.

In April some of the large-flowered hybrids will begin to bloom, those that bloom on old wood. Many colors are available—white, pink, blue and lavender—and many forms—ruffled, wavy, flat opened, doubles and singles. Some of these will rebloom in late summer or early fall.

Another group, hybrids from *C. alpina* and *C. macropetala,* also begin to bloom at this time. These are exquisite, thumb-sized bells that open flat above a petticoat of petaloid stamens. A little more difficult to find and more difficult to grow, they like a cooler site than other clematis. They come in shades of pinks and pale blues.

In May and June, the viticella and texensis hybrids bloom. *C. viticella,* although it has smaller flowers than the large-flowered hybrids (2 to 3 inches wide), it has them in greater profusion and for a longer time. The viticellas may be white, rose, blue, lavender and deep purple and some are even bicolored. This is one of the easiest clematis to grow and performs well as a companion to roses. The texensis group, originating from *C. texensis,* get their red color from that species and their down-facing bell shape, that can be flared or almost closed at the mouth. They are predominately pink, but a strong, warm pink that speaks out in the garden.

In July and August more of the large-flowered clematis will bloom and some that bloomed earlier may rebloom. One of the wonders of this time is the white-flowered *C. dioscoreifolia* that is completely covered with myriads of small, white flowers. Commonly called the sweet autumn clematis (although it blooms here in mid to late summer) *C. dioscoreifolia* has several synonyms. Often found locally as *C. maximowicziana,* it's also named *C. terniflora* and sometimes *C. paniculata.* Covered with a multitude of sweet-smelling foamy flowers, this clematis is a welcome sight in the heat of summer. Prune it almost completely to the ground in late winter; it grows 10 to 15 feet in a season.

Clematis texensis

As fall comes, the orange peel clematis, *C. orientalis* and *C. tangutica,* begin to bloom. The thick, yellow sepals give these species their name. This group makes wonderfully attractive seed heads that last in arrangements and wreaths for many months so that you can have a bit of clematis all through the winter.

The native species, *C. lasiantha,* and *C. ligusticifolia,* are drought-tolerant and once established, require no special soil or care. They are especially appropriate for native shrub areas where little care is needed and they can clamber through the bushes and even trees.

C. lasiantha, virgin's bower or pipestem clematis, can be found growing in chaparral from the Sierra Nevada foothills to Baja California. Its clusters of cream–white flowers in early spring are followed by fluffy clusters of feathery–tailed seedheads that last into fall. It is easily grown from seed or half–woody cuttings.

The petioles of the 3–parted leaves twist to help the vine cling or climb. Some of the bare, ropy branches may be pruned out or shortened in very early spring to control sprawl or for good flower production.

C. ligusticifolia, yerba de chevato, is similar to *C. lasiantha,* except that the slightly fragrant blooms are small, but in bigger clusters. However, the long-tailed seeds are not as crowded so the seed "ball" is not as attractive. It blooms later—late spring and into summer—and likes somewhat cooler areas. It is more often found growing along streambanks rather than open chaparral.

C. ligusticifolia blooms on previous year's wood, and should be cut back after blooming. It is grown from seed or half–woody cuttings.

Pruning a clematis properly requires that you know whether it is the sort that blooms on the previous year's wood or the current year's. For the former, prune only enough to maintain the framework of the vine. For the latter, prune severely in late winter to two or three nodes about 18 inches from the ground. Usually pruning instructions come with the plant. If not, there are several reference books devoted to clematis. Or you can just observe your vine: if flowers appear in the early spring, it is blooming on old wood. But if only new vegetative growth appears in spring and flowers bloom in the early summer, you have the second kind. The importance of keeping the new wood–bearing vines pruned each year is that left to their own devices, clematis will climb as high as possible and only the neighbors upstairs will ever get to see the flowers.

EG, MC, DR

Clematis texensis achene

CLYTOSTOMA CALLISTEGIOIDES (BIGNONIA VIOLACEA)
Bignoniaceae
Violet trumpet vine
Evergreen perennial

Clytostoma callistegioides, the violet or lavender trumpet vine, is still sometimes sold as *Bignonia violacea*. It is probably the hardiest of the tropical trumpet vines. Tops are hardy to 20 degrees, roots to 10 degrees.

Plants climb rapidly by tendrils to nearly any height support will allow. Tendrils form at the ends of the two leaflets that form each individual leaf. Branch ends trail when support is no longer available, and a characteristic plant will suspend a curtain of hanging stems from its horizontal framework stretching along eaves or fence.

Flowers appear from late spring until fall; they are 3 inches long, trumpet–shaped, with yellowish tube and flaring lavender bells with deep purple markings.

Its best use is as an eyebrow along eaves or fence; it is also useful for covering a pergola or other overhead structure. Its vigor makes it a good candidate for covering steep banks.

It can tolerate moderate shade, but blooms most heavily when given full sun, along with average soil and water. Prune heavily, shortening most growth in early spring and cutting back over–long shoots at any time.

DD

Clytostoma calistegioides

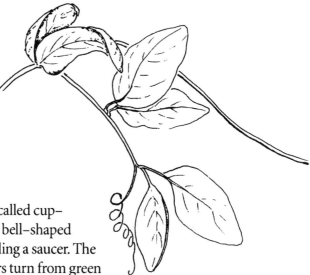

COBAEA SCANDENS
Polemoniaceae
CUP-AND-SAUCER VINE
Annual

Cobaea scandens is called cup–and–saucer vine because its bell–shaped flowers sit in a calyx resembling a saucer. The calyx is green, but the flowers turn from green to a purple–violet with both colors appearing on the plant at the same time.

Its origin in Central and South America makes it a tender plant, but if it freezes, another can be grown to flowering in a season. Grown from seed started indoors and transplanted outdoors when weather warms, it will grow vigorously to 25 feet on a trellis or pergola. In warmer climates than the Peninsula, it will grow to 40 feet. It needs regular water during its vigorous growth period.

Cup–and–saucer vine climbs by means of tendrils in the leaf axils. Leaves are paired oval leaflets, 4 inches long.

A specimen decorated the trellis at the end of the UC Cooperative Extension's kitchen garden at Gamble Gardens in 1995.

JW

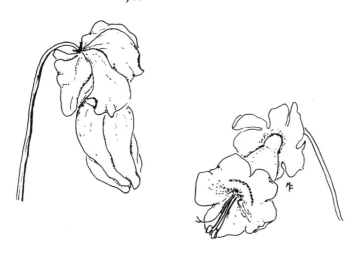

Cobaea scandens bud, stem, and flower

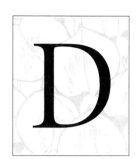

DISTICTIS BUCCINATORIA (BIGNONIA CHERERE, PHAEDRANTHUS BUCCINATORIUM)
Bignoniaceae
BLOOD-RED TRUMPET VINE
Evergreen perennial

The blood–red trumpet vine, *Distictis buccinatoria,* is a native of Mexico and will succumb to temperatures below 24 degrees. In a bright, sheltered location it will bloom sporadically throughout the summer. Its flowers are orange–red (rather than blood–red) trumpets, 4 inches long, with yellow–lined tubes. They fade to a bluish–red.

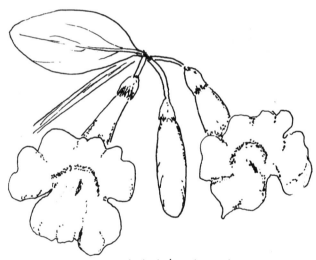

Distictis buccinatoria

Blood–red trumpet vine climbs by means of tendrils emerging from axils of the long, ovate leaflets. Mine grows on a fence and makes a spectacular entry display.

It needs water and fertilizer to get established, but once it gets going, this vigorous trumpet vine requires little summer water. Prune annually.

EL

DOLICHOS LABLAB (LABLAB PURPUREUS)
Fabaceae
HYACINTH BEAN
Annual

Thomas Jefferson grew hyacinth beans at Monticello. They are worth growing for their edible and pretty flowers, and edible pods and seeds.

Like string beans, hyacinth beans should be started from seed sown directly in the ground when the soil is fully warmed up in spring. Water deeply, but infrequently, to avoid mildew. It climbs by tendrils to 20 feet.

The flowers are a mauve–purple and the unusually–shaped seed pods a deep burgundy–purple.

An exciting combination on the same trellis or fence is hyacinth bean with its purple pods and flowers with scarlet runner bean with its bright orange–red flowers.

MB

DREGEA SINENSIS (WATTAKAKA SINENSIS)
Asclepiadaceae
CLIMBING MILKWEED
Deciduous, perennial

Climbing milkweed is a small climber that should be viewed up close to take in the honey scent of its star-shaped waxy white flowers with pink dots similar to the hoya to which it is related. Mine twines happily to the top of a rose arch where the flat flower umbels hang down to tempt the nose.

The leaves are felted and variegated in gray-green and cream colors. It loses its leaves in winter and requires filtered shade and regular water.

Western Hills Rare Plant Nursery is one source of the plant.

SA

ECCREMOCARPUS SCABER
Bignoniaceae
CHILEAN GLORY FLOWER
Evergreen perennial

Although Chilean glory flower is a native to Chile and Argentina, it is hardy and evergreen on the Peninsula. My experience does not include growing it in temperatures below 15 degrees. The plants grow rapidly from seed and will begin to flower within five months. When established, the plant is in flower from early spring to fall.

Hummingbirds are drawn to the lovely and abundant sprays of soft, salmon–colored flowers. Each individual flower is slightly pouch–shaped, tubular and about 1 inch long. The vine creates a light, delicate appearance and grows to about 10 feet.

Chilean glory flower's fine tendrils are able to cling to rough stucco or a netting support, but not to a solid board fence. The black plastic wire used for keeping off birds works well. Sometimes open shrubbery can serve as a support if the vine is trained into it. The plant needs some sun, but not all day. Morning sun, or lightly filtered sun with some direct sun is fine. The plant has a habit of occasionally looking as if it has died. Don't take it out. New growth can again originate from dead–looking trunks and stems.

When possible, plant the seed indoors in a seed pan in February or March. Cover seeds very lightly with soil, using a sterile potting mix. Set seed pots in a pan of water until surface of soil is wet.

Germination normally takes two weeks or less. When seedlings begin to appear, place seed pan where it will receive a few hours of sun daily or else the seedlings will become spindly. Transplant to individual pots when true leaves appear. When young plants are 6 to 8 inches high, plant in a permanent place in the garden. Be sure to bait for snails and slugs.

Add mulch to garden soil when you plant and disturb seedling roots as little as possible. Do not keep in containers too long.

The seeds germinate readily and you will probably have several plants. Because the plant is rare, you may find several friends who will appreciate receiving those you cannot use—and more hummingbirds will be nourished.

LB

Eccremocarpus scaber

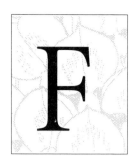

FATSHEDERA
Araliaceae
BOTANICAL WONDER, IVY TREE, ARALIA IVY
Evergreen perennial

Fatshedera is a cross between *Fatsia japonica* and *Hedera hibernica* in the Araliaceae family. It is of garden origin and occurred in France in 1910.

More a lax shrub than a vine, the stems must be tied to a support to keep them in place. Green plants of this hybrid can be made into pleasing patterns on a large shady wall or fence, growing to 10 feet or more. One variegated selection has green leaves with creamy edges. A third selection has gold and yellow markings on a dark green leaf. Because of the coloring this selection is a favorite for use in flower arrangements.

The palmate leaves have five points much like large ivy leaves that may grow to 5 inches across. Seldom branching, this vine should be headed back while young to develop several leaders , depending upon how it is to be used.

EC

FICUS PUMILA
Moraceae
CREEPING FIG
Evergreen perennial

Creeping fig (*Ficus pumila*, more often sold as *F. repens*), is more familiar to Bay Area gardeners in commercial settings than in home gardens. It is the fine–textured evergreen vine that makes a delicate tracery against the shaded masonry walls of large buildings in shopping centers. In this, its juvenile phase, its leaves are tiny and neatly arranged along slender stems that cling by means of aerial roots. It will maintain this pattern if cut back occasionally to the ground. If given its head, it will cover any given surface with a dense blanket of larger (2 to 4 inches) leathery leaves borne on short, stout branches that stand out straight from the wall and will in time produce inedible 2 1/2-inch, pear-shaped or cylindrical figs.

This vine can make a very attractive pattern on a masonry wall; it should not be planted on wooden surfaces that may need repainting, nor on shingles; even on masonry it should be cut back hard whenever it exceeds the wanted pattern or shows signs of mature growth (large leaves, stiff horizontal branches). It will not thrive on a hot south or west wall. Water needs are average, and stored heat in its wall usually keeps it from frost damage.

DD, FA

GELSEMIUM SEMPERVIRENS
Loganiaceae
CAROLINA JESSAMINE
Evergreen perennial

Carolina jessamine (*Gelsemium sempervirens*), an evergreen vine in the Logania (or Buddleia) family (Loganiaceae), is notable for fresh-looking, shiny green foliage and bright yellow flowers in late winter or early spring. It grows by twining to a height of 20 feet or less at a moderate rate. Oval, paired leaves are 1 to 4 inches long and the fragrant funnel–shaped flowers are bright yellow, their color heightened by an orange center.

Blooming period is late winter or early spring. Plants require average garden water and routine feeding. Native to the southern parts of the U. S. and Mexico, it is hardy anywhere in the Bay Area.

Uses are many; they can climb a trellis or post (the latter may require some initial tying in), cover a chain link fence, or trail along the eaves, dropping a curtain of flowering streamers. I have observed many twining around guy wires of utility poles; they make these hazards to navigation more readily visible, as well as prettier.

Flowers are rich in nectar, but this should not be sipped; it is poisonous and can be deadly, like all other parts of this relative of the plant that produces strychnine.

DD

HARDENBERGIA
Fabaceae
Evergreen perennial

Hardenbergia comptoniana and *Hardenbergia violacea* are Australian evergreen twining vines in the Pea family. The former comes from Western Australia and is less widely grown than the latter because it is less hardy to frost; temperatures in the lower 20's may kill it to the ground. It can reach 9 or 10 feet, with equal spread. Leaves are divided into 3 to 5 narrow 2 to 3–inch–long leaflets. Long, narrow clusters of violet–blue, pea-shaped flowers form in late winter or spring. A choice vine with fine–textured foliage and attractive flowers, it is rarely seen, although it has been in California nurseries for many years.

H. violacea, also widely sold as *H. monophylla*, is hardier to frost and far more common. Its leaves are undivided, narrowly egg-shaped, dark green, 2 to 4 inches long. Vines are vigorous and fast growing, and the flower clusters at branch ends are heavily produced. Colors range from purple to (rarely) pink or white. The pinkish-purple cultivated variety, 'Happy Wanderer', is exceptionally vigorous and is the one commonly offered in nurseries. The pink cultivar 'Rosea' is available.

Hardenbergias like sun, but tolerate light shade. They can endure some drought, but do better with ample water. Prune right after bloom to control growth; hard pruning will benefit old, tangled plants.

Use on trellis or pillar, or peg down as ground cover.

DD, CM

HEDERA
Araliaceae
Ivy
Evergreen perennial

The ivies (*Hedera*) are true vines, but have been so widely used in the West as ground cover that their vinelike qualities are often overlooked. Indeed, ivy growing on a tree is a potential pest; its foliage can shade out that of its host and its roots can steal water and nutrients. Still, ivy in its place can be extremely useful. It presents a uniform appearance throughout the year, with no highs or lows; it is easily trained into formal shapes; and it is tough, asking little except protection from the hottest sun in hot climates, and a modicum of water.

English ivy *(H. helix)* is by far the commonest species, and it can be had in dozens of cultivated varieties. To see them all, visit the North Coast Botanical Garden just south of Fort Bragg; it houses the national collection in a special shade house. All are accurately named and beautifully displayed. The most commonly used in gardens as a ground cover or a vine is 'Baltica', which has small, dull, dark green leaves with pale veins. Like other ivies it climbs by holdfast aerial roots which cling to any surface. (Beware of planting it against a surface that needs occasional repainting.) 'Baltica' is useful to form a tracery or a cover on masonry walls or to conceal a lamp post or mailbox support. Stems may also be led along wires to create formal espalier patterns.

Even better for this sort of filigree work are the smaller-leafed, finely-cut cultivated varieties such as 'Minima', 'Needlepoint', and 'Pedata' (bird's foot ivy). All these are effective clinging to balustrades, urns, statuary, or masonry stairs and walls. These are also naturals for shaping into topiary forms. Particularly showy is 'Goldheart', a small-leafed dark green ivy with a bright yellow patch in the center of each leaf. It is restrained in growth habit and is eye-catching climbing an old tree trunk.

Hedera helix 'Gold Heart'

H. canariensis and its green and white variety 'Variegata' are splashy plants with large, glossy leaves. Coarser than English ivy, they are used principally as ground cover, although any of them can be trained to a pillar or displayed along a wall. They need more water than English ivy and the variegated form can suffer in heat and drought.

DD

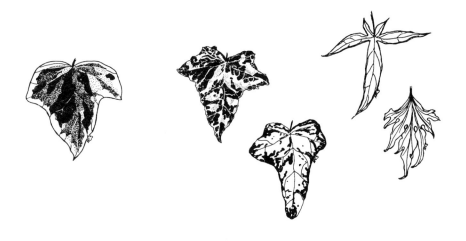

H. helix 'Gold Dust'   *H. helix 'Calico'*   *H. helix 'Itsy Bitsy'*
(previous page: H. helix 'Itsy Bitsy' spray)

HIBBERTIA SCANDENS
Dilleniaceae
GUINEA GOLD VINE
Evergreen perennial

Hibbertia scandens is the only member of its genus commonly grown in the Bay Area, although several of its smaller relatives show great promise as rock garden plants or shrubs. We call it Guinea gold vine; in its native Australia it is commonly called climbing Guinea flower. Capable of reaching 15 feet in height, it is usually seen to be much lower here.

Hibbertia's twining stems have a good cover of thickish, shiny, dark green leaves that make a good background for the large (2 to 3–inch) bright yellow flowers, which have the look of single wild roses. Bloom season is spring to late fall, but some flowers may appear at any time of the year.

It thrives best in a sunny place with good drainage, but can take light shade. Here we use it to display on a fence, trellis, or pillar; Australians use it as a ground or bank cover. Without support it sprawls. Australian sources credit it with high tolerance of seashore conditions and use it as dune planting. It might not do so well in our cold, foggy coastal conditions. Heavy frost can damage it, but recovery is fast.

DD

HOYA CARNOSA
Asclepiadaceae
WAX FLOWER
Evergreen perennial

Hoya carnosa

Hoya carnosa is a deep green, evergreen sturdy vine, grown outdoors in overhead protected, mild areas, or as a houseplant or greenhouse plant on trellis. The sturdy, opposite leaves, with short, thick petioles, are 3 to 4 inches long. Wax flower belongs to the milkweed family, the tight umbel of 1/2–inch waxy flowers showing the relationship.

Hoya is summer-blooming, flowers are creamy-white with a 5–pointed crimson "star" in the center. Do not cut off flower stems when cluster withers; new flower umbels grow from the old flower stems. It blooms best when plant becomes pot–bound.

Plant hoya in loose, well–drained soil. If outdoors, keep on dry side during cool months. It does well in hanging pots, where the long shoots can hang or be looped around supporting wires.

MC

HUMULUS LUPULUS
Cannabaceae
HOP VINE
Deciduous perennial

The fruits of the hop vine, *Humulus lupulus,* are used to flavor beer, but it is also a fast–growing ornamental, twining plant that provides shade for a sunny wall or porch.

Because it is native to North America and Europe, the strong root system of hop vine will survive the coldest winters. It is best to cut it to the ground in fall when the leaves turn brown. In spring young leaves are toothed and entire but when mature, they are three–lobed and dark green. The leaves and hairy stems are rough to the touch.

Flowers develop toward the end of the current year's growth as a cluster of papery bracts at several of the leaf nodes. These are the "hops."

H. lupulus 'Aurea' is the most decorative of the hop vines. Its golden foliage is best when grown in nearly full sun.

For fast growth, hops should be well watered after growth starts in spring. New plants can be grown from cuttings or root divisions.
  EC

Humulus lupulus

HYDRANGEA SEEMANNII
Hydrangeaceae (Saxifragaceae)
EVERGREEN CLIMBING HYDRANGEA
Evergreen perennial

Hydrangea seemannii, as its common name suggests, doesn't lose its leaves in winter unlike the more commonly-known climbing hydrangea, *H. petiolaris*, although the white lacecap flowers are similar.

The most striking feature of this hydrangea is the golf ball size buds which open to a rounded corymb of 1–inch sterile flowers and many small white fertile flowers.

H. seemanii originates in Mexico, and its cold hardiness is unknown, although one specimen in Kentfield survived the 1990 freeze.

It can grow up to 3 feet a year, clinging like ivy by rootlets to walls and fences. The dark–green leathery leaves are attractive even when it is out of bloom. The foliage is sparse so it makes an outline on a fence.

It requires shade, rich soil and moderate water.

The evergreen climbing hydrangea is available from Western Hills Rare Plant Nursery, Occidental, but should be seen more frequently in the trade.

SA

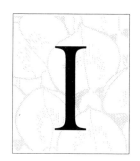

IPOMOEA
Convolvulaceae
MORNING GLORY
Deciduous perennial

Ipomoea nil is a tender perennial usually treated as an annual in our climate. It is an herbaceous twiner with hairy stems and leaves that may be heart–shaped or lobed. The sturdy stems grow very quickly and easily reach 8 to 10 feet.

I. nil includes several morning glories besides the well-known 'Imperial Japanese' morning glory. For example, there is the cultivar 'Scarlett O'Hara' which has rich crimson flowers and 'Limbata,' with purple flowers edged in white.

The flowers have traditionally been cultivated and especially bred for size and color by the Japanese; the tube of the funnelform flowers is as much as 2 1/2 inches long, the salverform corolla correspondingly large. A wide range of colors in the blues and reds as well as pure white is possible. One can sometimes tell the flower color early in a bunch of seedlings from the suffusion of color on the stem.

They are easily raised from seed if a few procedures are followed. The seed should be soaked in water overnight and those seeds that have swollen sown immediately. The seeds that have not imbibed water should be nicked or filed to breach the hard seed coat and soaked again before sowing.

It is traditional in Japan to grow them in pots, making a cylinder of blooming plants. These specially bred plants need plenty of water and regular feeding to realize their potential. The fertilizer of choice for the Japanese grower is rape–seed meal, the solid remains from which rape-seed oil is processed, but this is not readily available in garden centers so any complete fertilizer will probably do.

Ipomoea indica, blue dawn flower, has undergone two name changes in the last few decades; you will have better luck finding it if you look for it under its synonyms *I. leari* or *I. acuminata*. Three–inch flowers resemble those of the more familiar annual morning glories, but their color is unmistakable; a bright, deep blue with a white throat, aging to purplish pink. The blue is much deeper that than of the familiar 'Heavenly Blue' morning glory, but blooms of both contain an undertone of red that, although invisible to the naked eye, is easily caught by most color films, making a true rendering nearly impossible.

Plants grow rapidly by twining to a height of 20 to 30 feet, and old plants are capable of completely blanketing large shrubs or middle-sized trees, making spectacular if somewhat untidy spectacles. Plants are perennial, although they may lose leaves or die back nearly to the ground in harsh frost. Roots are hardy to about 15 degrees. Plants are not always easily available, but are being produced by several growers. They can tolerate poor soil so long as it is well drained and appreciate average garden watering. Use for screening or ground cover.

Ipomoea X multifida (Quamoclit X sloteri), cardinal climber, is an easily grown, but hard to find, annual vine. The foliage is lacy; the lovely small, abundant flowers are a strikingly brilliant red. It is an outstanding source of nectar for hummingbirds during its long season of bloom from earliest summer through late fall.

The 10 to 12–foot twining stems will wind around a trellis or open wire fencing. For it to climb a thick post, provide a support such as wide staples over the ascending stems. The plants like full sun, but grow well with sun only half a day.

Sow seeds indoors in late March, April or May. Soak the seeds two to three hours in warm water before planting two seeds in a 4–inch pot, one seed per smaller pot. Cover with 1/4–inch soil, water gently. Germination occurs in about a week.

Place outdoors in sun as soon as well up and night temperatures are above 40 degrees. When 6 to 8 inches tall, the plants are ready for the garden. Spade in humus and aged manure. Plant as growing in pot or carefully separate and space 10 inches or so apart.

Harvest cardinal climber seed in fall. This plant will not volunteer because the seeds disintegrate in our winter weather. If you can find others with whom to share some of your excess seed, you will bring pleasure to more hummingbirds—and people.

Ipomoea lobata (Mina lobata), flag of Spain, is a most unusual and attractive annual vine with the habit of a morning glory and twin spikes of tubular flowers, red in bud and maturing yellow. It's a real show stopper! Hummingbirds love it and it makes an unusual and long-lasting cut flower as well.

Sow the seed in early summer where the plants are to remain in full sun in the garden. When the weather is warm, poke the large seeds into the soil about 1/2-inch deep, firm the soil and keep the surface moist until germination takes place in about 10 to 15 days.

Indoors the seeds may be planted three or four to each 2-inch pot of seed-starting mix. Keep the seed pots in a bright window out of direct sun. When the seedlings have their first set of true leaves (the second apparent set of leaves), they may be moved outdoors to bright shade to harden off, then to their permanent location in the garden. Transplant carefully as they resent root disturbance.

EG, DD, LB

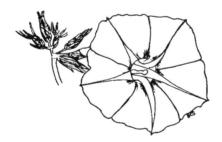

Ipomea indica

JASMINUM
Oleaceae
JASMINE
Evergreen perennial

Although it was introduced into gardens much later than common or true jasmine, *Jasminum officinale (J. polyanthum)* has certainly overtaken it (and any of the other jasmines) in the favor of bay area gardeners. It is as vigorous as the former (or more so) and is far more floriferous, opening clouds of small white blossoms from pinkish buds. The fragrance is legendary. The slender stems twine quickly around any given support to reach a height of 12 feet or more or (if unsupported) will sprawl along the ground and take root. The bright green leaves have 5 to 7 leaflets, and the flowers are carried in branched clusters from the axils of the upper leaves, making sheafs of bloom.

This vine will survive with very little summer water, but is more luxuriant with ample water and sunlight. It is so vigorous that it will need considerable cutting back after bloom if it is not to become an unmanageable tangle. Growth is quick, and a gallon–sized plant (easily obtainable at any nursery) will make a sizable vine within the year. It can take heavy pruning, and plants growing in hanging baskets can be pinched to make attractive arching cascades of late winter or early spring bloom. Plants so treated will flower well indoors in cool, bright rooms and, of course, also on deck or patio.

Dick Dunmire's plant shares a front porch post with a large-flowered clematis, which it would overwhelm if not cut back hard after bloom. (He does not recommend the combination; it is attractive over a long season, but the vines tangle and present pruning problems.)

Jasminum nitidum, (J. magnificum), angelwing jasmine, grows rather slowly to 10–20 feet. It needs a warm location and a long growing season to bloom well, but Roz Bray's on a south-facing fence sunburns easily. Semi-deciduous, it has fragrant, white flowers with purple underneath in early summer.

Jasminum grandiflorum, Spanish jasmine, grows well in the Bay Area. After Sherry Austin's froze to 18 inches in the Yukon Express of 1990, it came back with a vengeance to its usual 10 to 20 feet.

The small, white star–shaped flowers are most profuse in spring although there are some flowers most of the year. It is most valued for its fragrance and indeed, this species is the one from which jasmine perfume is made.

The shrubby vine is thought to be from between Iran to China, along the trading routes, but its country of origin is still uncertain. We do know it made its way to Britain as early as 1548.

It is not particular about the soil in which its grows, takes part shade and average water.

Sherry Austin's is trained to the top of a wall over which its arching branches spill.

SA, DD, RB

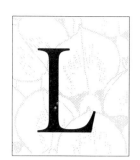

LAPAGERIA ROSEA
Liliaceae
CHILEAN BELLFLOWER
Evergreen perennial

The Chilean bellflower (*Lapageria rosea*) sends up wiry stems that can reach 20 feet with adequate support. Thickest stems from the root system are no larger than finger diameter; these branch in an unpredictable manner into thin, tough stems that support leathery, glossy, oval pointed leaves up to 5 inches long. Flowers, which appear from midsummer through winter, droop from leaf axils along the upper ends of branchlets and cluster in bunches of 2 to 5 at branchlet ends.

The vine tends to be a tangled ugly duckling, but it can be forgiven because of its thick–textured, waxy, 6–petaled flowers that betray its distant relationship to the lilies. These are typically bell–shaped, drooping, 3 inches long, rose–red, marbled within with pale or whitish pink and white.

Lapageria is rare because of its slow growth and difficulty of propagation; cuttings are said to be possible. Seeds are hard to find (plants are apparently not self-pollinating or only slightly so) and must be sown when absolutely fresh. A note in a recent issue of *The New Plantsman* suggests slitting open the seed pod and planting it entire, pulp and all, then separating the seedlings as they begin to grow. Young plants grow very slowly at first, but established plants send out long, quick–growing stems. I once divided a pot-grown specimen of the white–flowered, cultivated variety 'White Cloud' for a friend who "had to have one". My half is still alive but resentful; it has made little growth in the last 5 years, although it shows an occasional flower. The friend's plant? His dog ate it within a week.

Lapageria rosea bud

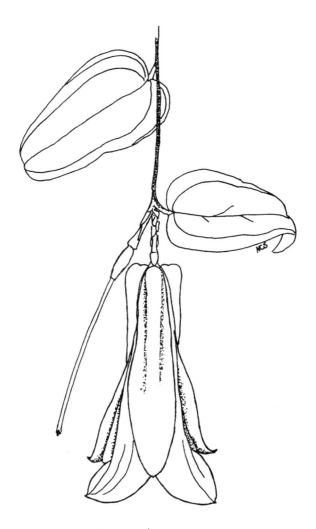

Lapageria rosea

It likes shade and a cool root run. My 40-year old plant grows along a wall on the northeast side of the house, with most of the root system under a wooden deck. It receives one feeding with acid plant food each year in spring and is soaked once a week during warm weather. Frost has never damaged it, possibly because it has radiated heat of the house wall. Pruning is needed only to prevent tangling, but some grooming is necessary; this consists in pulling off withered flowers.

Chileans have named this their national flower; their name for it is copihue (co'-pe-way). It is native to forests in the cool, moist southern part of their country.

DD

LONICERA
Caprifoliaceae
HONEYSUCKLE
Deciduous perennial

Honeysuckles will grow in a wide range of soil types, but prefer deep, humus–rich soil (what doesn't?). They are shallow rooted and don't like hot, sunbaked soil. They require regular water, but no fertilizer.

Gold net honeysuckle, *Lonicera japonica* 'Aureoreticulata', is grown for its beautiful, gold–veined leaves. In Sherry Austin's garden, it twines on a rose arch with a *Solanum crispum* 'Glasnevin' where its leaves spark up the green of the potato vine.

Both tolerate heavy pruning a couple times a year to keep them under control. Both are deciduous, take part shade, average soil and regular water.

Woodbine, *Lonicera periclymenum*, is regarded for its large, fragrant flowers which appear from May to August. In fall it produces large numbers of bright red berries. 'Serotina,' in Roz Bray's garden, has profuse yellow and pinkish–purple flowers. Another cultivar, 'Belgica,' is said to flower earlier and has creamier flowers.

Once established, woodbine seems to like heavy pruning in the spring. Indeed, it will grow into a large, shrubby clump if left untrained. Roz trained hers over a trellis and whacks it back whenever it gets unruly.

Woodbine is native to Europe and North Africa, but is easy to grow on the Peninsula. It will root easily from hardwood cuttings taken in October or November.

Among mail order sources of *L. periclymenum* 'Serotina' and other honeysuckles are ForestFarm and Wayside Gardens.

RB, SA

LYCIANTHES RANTONNEI (SOLANUM RANTONNEI)
Solanaceae
PARAGUAY NIGHTSHADE, BLUE POTATO BUSH
Evergreen perennial

Paraguay nightshade or blue potato bush (*Lycianthes rantonnei*, often sold as *Solanum rantonnei*) is commonly seen as a shrub or small standard tree, but it is by nature a vine that can climb to 15 feet if given support and a little tying–in to get it started.

The vines bloom profusely over a long period. The clusters of blue, 2 to 5 inch–wide, flowers with bright yellow centers appear throughout warm weather, sometimes throughout the year. Bright green oval leaves to 4 inches long are ordinarily evergreen, but may drop in unusually cold winters, and occasionally branch tips will die back, but recovery is fast.

This plant is extremely showy at close range because of the profusion and long season of bloom. Curiously enough, it is not so showy at a distance; the leaves and flowers have about the same depth of color, and the flowers tend to blend with the foliage. Plant it near a pathway or seating area for best effect.

Tree-shaped plants 6 to 10 feet tall and as wide have been staked, thinned of their lower branches, and frequently pinched to produce a dense head. Plant habit depends on training; plants may even sprawl as ground cover if desired.

Two flower colors are commonly seen. *Lycianthes rantonnei* generally has flowers on the blue side of violet. However, the selected cultivated variety 'Royal Robe' has flowers on the red–purple side.

DD

MACFADYENA UNGUIS-CATI
Bignoniaceae
CAT'S CLAW, YELLOW TRUMPET VINE
Semi-evergreen perennial

Ironically, this aggressive, rapidly–growing climber (to 25–40 feet) looks rather wispy as its growing tips curl outward from the body of the plant. Contributing to its delicate presentation are the 2–inch, foxglove–like, yellow flowers and the oval, glossy green leaves, both of which are smaller than those of the lavender and blood–red trumpet vines. A spectacular flower display occurs in May followed by attractive, pendulous brown–black seed pods.

Although this vine is reported to be partly deciduous, Scott Loosley, the horticulturist at Gamble Garden in Palo Alto, recalls only slight damage to the leaves during the severe freeze of 1990. At Gamble, the vine provides a dense cover to an arbor adjacent to the tea house and covers a low fence on the south side of the wisteria garden. A cat's claw in Los Gatos covers a brick wall 20 feet by 40 feet.

The vine should be pruned aggressively soon after flowering since it flowers on old wood. In addition, it profits from a major renovation every five years or so, according to Scott Loosley.

This native of Mexico, the West Indies, and Central and South America can withstand full sun or partial shade and aridity. It attaches to any surface with its tiny, three-pronged claws.

NM

MANDEVILLA LAXA (MANDEVILLA SUAVEOLENS)
Apocynaceae
CHILEAN JASMINE
Deciduous perennial

Chilean jasmine is fast growing with wonderful, fragrant white trumpet-shaped flowers. Mine climbed to the top of the arbor from a one-gallon can in just one season. The oval leaves are about 4 inches long. It likes sun, rich soil and lots of water.

It is hardy to at least 15 degrees and the roots to 5 degrees. Chilean jasmine needs to be cut back hard every winter. It blooms on new growth.

Grow it in a place where the fragrance will be enjoyed frequently. Watch out for spider mites.

SA

METROSIDEROS CARMINEUS
Myrtaceae
Evergreen perennial

Metrosideros carmineus is a climbing species in the same genus as the New Zealand Christmas tree. If planted out in the open this plant will make a ground cover with fine branches and very small round leaves. When planted next to a tree it will climb like an ivy. A 40–foot vine was reported in New Zealand.

Upon reaching the top of a support it will develop adult foliage and then produce the beautiful carmine flowers in dense terminal clusters. Most effective if trained up a pole of about 6 feet where the flowers can be seen to the best advantage. If cuttings are made from the adult foliage a compact pot plant can be developed.

As an understory vine, this *Metrosideros* should be grown in part shade. It takes regular water and any good garden soil. It is hardy in all but the most severe frosts or where the ground freezes.

It is not common, but may be found in plant sales at Strybing Arboretum, San Francisco.

EC

MOMORDICA CHARANTIA
Cucurbitaceae
BITTER MELON, BALSAM PEAR
Annual

Bitter melon, *Momordica charantia*, is an annual heat–loving vine which will grow to about 10 feet with moderate amounts of water and lots of sun. On the Peninsula it is slow to start if spring is cool, but it comes into its own with late summer heat.

The leaves are delicately cut, palmately lobed and an attractive light green. It climbs by wrapping tendrils around twigs, bamboo stakes or other thin support.

The small, yellow flowers are inconspicuous compared to the gourd–like fruits which are 4 to 6 inches long, pale green and very warty. As the fruits ripen, they turn yellow, then pale orange and split open along the length revealing bright red, shiny seeds. These are most striking to see on the vine. Many Asian people use the fruit in the kitchen, especially in soup and for stir-frying.

The vine grows easily from seed as long as the soil is really warm and moist.

Some mail order sources for the seed of bitter melon are: Thompson and Morgan, Park Seed Company, and Nichols Garden Nursery.

RB

MUEHLENBECKIA COMPLEXA
Polygonaceae
MATTRESS VINE, WIRE VINE
Evergreen perennial

Muehlenbeckia complexa is in Polygonaceae and a native of New Zealand. The common name of mattress or wire vine is the perfect name for this thin, wiry-stemmed plant. If planted out in the open it can make a tangled mass of wiry stems and tiny green leaves. It could be used as a cover for a wire fence or trained on an old stump as a standard.

The flowers are no bigger than 1/4–inch, white and shaped like a cup. Fruits are small white, translucent berries enclosing tiny black seeds, and occur in fall.

As a ground cover wire vine can be invasive and must have plenty of space. It will do well in part shade or full sun with little care. It is considered a novelty or collector's plant.

EC

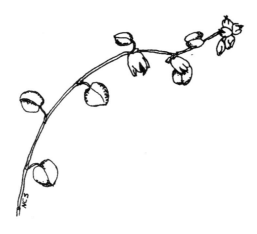

Muehlenbeckia complexa

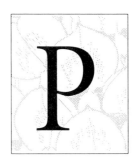

PANDOREA
Bignoniaceae
BOWER VINE, WONGA-WONGA VINE
Evergreen perennial

Two species of *Pandorea*, one of the many genera in the Bignonia family (Bignoniaceae) are to be found in Bay Area gardens; both have exceedingly attractive glossy foliage, and both have attractive flowers which, though similar in structure, are much unlike in color and form. Both tolerate full sun in coolest areas, but appreciate some shade it hot locations. They thrive in average good garden soil with moderate watering.

The better known is *Pandorea jasminoides*, bower vine, which is the showier of the two and the more tender, being subject to severe damage in hard or prolonged frosts. It twines quickly to 20 to 30 feet, but can be restrained by pinching and pruning. Shiny bright green leaves are divided into five to nine 1 to 2-inch leaflets. The 2- inch, trumpet-shaped flowers come in clusters at branch ends and are typically white with pink throats. The cultivated varieties 'Alba' and 'Lady Di' have pure white flowers, while 'Rosea' has pink flowers with deep rose throats. Blooms are evident from early summer to mid-autumn, but the plant is attractive at all seasons. Give it a sheltered spot to protect it against frost and cold or drying winds.

Less common, but becoming more available in nurseries, is *P. pandorana*, wonga-wonga vine. Somewhat hardier to frost and equally attractive in foliage, the eastern Australia native has clusters of spring flowers less than 1-inch long. They are whitish or creamy yellow, usually heavily spotted with brownish-purple.

DD

PARTHENOCISSUS
Vitaceae
VIRGINIA CREEPER, BOSTON IVY
Deciduous perennial

Parthenocissus quinquefolia, Virginia creeper, is a familiar sight on masonry buildings and walls where its bold foliage softens and covers architectural starkness. This vine clings to rough surfaces by means of holdfasts that develop from adhesive discs on the tips of the tendrils.

The bold, handsome leaves are palmately compound with five coarsely–toothed leaflets. As the vine matures and covers the wall with a dense mat of stems, the leaves are borne on short branchlets that arch out displaying the leaves in overlapping fashion. The foliage, which is deciduous, tends to be purplish when just opening in the spring, matures to green in summer, then turns brilliant red in fall. It is only fair to add that the color is better in areas when night and day temperatures in autumn are sharply contrasting.

Virginia creeper is slow to get started, although its later growth rate is rapid. Spraying or misting the wall on which the vine is to grow is said to encourage the speed with which the vine gets established.

It makes a very effective ground cover, rooting at the joints as it travels. Inconspicuous flowers are borne on lateral branchlets, developing into clusters of blue-black berries on red stalks. The flowers are attractive to bees in late summer.

This is a large and vigorous vine with 3 to 6–inch leaves and needs a large canvas. There are disadvantages to growing it on wooden structures that may need to be painted because the holdfasts are nearly impossible to remove from wood.

Boston ivy, *Parthenocissus tricuspidata,* resembles Virginia creeper in being a tenacious wall covering vine but differs in being a more densely–growing species. The leaves have 3 sharply-pointed, coarsely-serrate lobes. The upper surface is shiny, bright green and the leaves persist on the vine here, but are deciduous in colder climates.

Boston ivy spreads widely from the base, fanning out in all directions and clinging tightly to almost any surface. It makes a thick mat against a wall. The leaves are small at first, but increasing in size with age, are on long petioles that stand away from the wall. In colder areas, fall color adds to the attractiveness of Boston ivy, and there are several available varieties that feature different color variants. A smaller-leaved variety, 'Veitchii', has ovate or trifoliate leaves that are purple when young.

Parthenocissus henryana, silver–veined creeper, is a smaller, more refined version of Virginia creeper with five-toothed leaflets that have the added and elegant touch of silvery–white midribs and veins. This one also has outstanding fall color when leaves turn a rich red. In summer its leaf clusters are dark green with silver veining on top and reddish–purple underneath with garnet–colored stems. It climbs quickly to more than five feet on tendrils with suction cups. It is not as vigorous as the more common Virginia creeper or Boston ivy and doesn't cling as tenaciously.

The color is best in shade. Too much sun is said to promote red spider mites.

Silver-veined creeper will climb a shady wall although it can be grown in pots if you have the heart to cut down the beautiful leaves annually. In a pot you can see both the top and bottom of the leaves. Filoli grows this ivy on many of its brick walls.

Good drainage is required and regular water.

EG, SA, JF

PASSIFLORA
Passifloraceae
PASSION VINE
Semi-evergreen perennial

There are more than 500 species in Passifloraceae: vines, shrubs and small trees. The majority of these are grown for the colorful intricate flowers and fast growth to provide shade.

Passiflora edulis has the classic intricate flower with many wavy filaments, white with purple bands. Fruits are 2 to 3 inches, round to oblong in shape and can be purple or yellow in color. This berry has a hard thick rind that encloses many seeds each in an individual envelope of pulp and juice which makes up about 30% of the weight. When fully ripe the fruit will show wrinkles and if left on the vine will drop to the ground where they may be gathered. These may be cut in half and eaten out of the rind or scooped out and frozen until enough pulp has been collected for drinks or a pie!

The purple-fruited passion vine is most common in our area while the yellow, which is less hardy, is grown where there are no frosts. This vine has 3-lobed leaves carried on rather angular stems and supported by strong tendrils from the leaf nodes. Passiflora can be successfully grown on a wire support consisting of several horizontal wires about 18 inches apart and 8 to 10 feet long. The main canes should be tied to the wires to make a modified espalier. Side spurs will develop from the horizontal canes which will bear the fruit. The fruiting spurs should be cut back almost to the main canes in the early spring to prevent the plant from becoming overgrown.

This native of Brazil should have good drainage and a sunny warm protected spot. *P. edulis* may be propagated by seeds or cuttings taken almost any time of the year. Not long lived, this passiflora should be replaced with new vines every 4 or 5 years. Except for snails it is rather free of insects and will create a lush tropical background for other plantings or help shade a sunny wall while flowering and fruiting all summer.

Passiflora alata-caerulea

P. alata-caerulea (P. pfordtii) has inedible bulb-shaped fruits, but is grown for its outstanding, semi-fragrant, 3 to 4-inch flowers which appear from spring to early fall. The blooms are stunning as corsages or centerpiece floaters.

Passiflora alata-caerulea

The hybrid 'Lavender Lady' combines the best characteristics of its parents, *P. amethystina* and *P. caerulea*. Closely branched and covered solidly with dark blue–green, 3–lobed leaves, its 4–inch flowers are produced continuously with peaks in spring and fall. The outer segments have reddish-violet margins shading to nearly white centers, while the inner segments are lavender. The corona combines bands of purple, white and deep maroon. It was undamaged by 20 degree temperatures in 1990. This hybrid is available and can be ordered by your local nursery from Suncrest wholesalers.

The genus name derives from biblical analogies. One follows— the ten colored sepals and petals represent the ten apostles present at the crucifixion; the five orange stamens, the five wounds of Christ, and the purple filaments, the crown of thorns.

A southern, full sun exposure, preferably adjacent to a wall enables this hybrid to grow well on the Peninsula. Root-hardy and semi-evergreen, it loses 30 to 50% of its leaves in mild winters. A fast–growing climber to 25 or 35 feet, the old or tangled foliage should be clipped in winter.

Passion vine will abide a wide range of soils and conditions and requires only moderate water and fertilizer. It has few pest problems.

EC, DH

PHASEOLUS COCCINEA
Fabaceae
SCARLET RUNNER BEAN
Perennial treated as annual

Scarlet runner bean is not only ornamental,but has the added advantage of having edible fruit and flowers. Even the starchy, carrot–like root is edible, if not especially choice.

Before the fruit (bean) appears on the pole bean plant, there are orangey–red flowers that attract hummingbirds. They are attractive in green salads or as a garnish in soup.

When the bean pods are small and young, they can be cooked and eaten like regular string beans. As the seeds enlarge, they can be removed from pods and cooked like fresh lima beans. In maturity, the large, one–inch seeds are speckled black and purple and can be used as dry beans.

Scarlet runner beans prefer full sun and good garden loam, but are fairly tolerant of poor soil. To avoid mildew, water infrequently, but deeply.

A native of South America, scarlet runner bean roots will overwinter in mild winter areas and above–ground growth will return the following warm season, although performance is inferior to the prior year.

MB

PHILADELPHUS MEXICANUS
Hydrangeaceae (Saxifragaceae)
EVERGREEN MOCK ORANGE
Evergreen perennial

The evergreen mock orange is a shrubby vine that is appropriate for the old–fashioned or woodland garden.

Fairly fast growing, it attains 15 to 20 feet in a few years. Mine hangs down from the tree it has climbed, and the creamy blossoms occur on the growth tips in the sun. The fragrant, orange blossom smell tantalizes the garden visitor in spring when the double, 1 1/2–inch flowers are most abundant.

The vine requires no pruning and is cold hardy, since it came though the 1990 freeze with no damage.

A single form can be ordered from Suncrest through retail nurseries.

MK

PLUMBAGO AURICULATA (PLUMBAGO CAPENSIS)
Plumbaginaceae
CAPE PLUMBAGO
Semi-evergreen perennial

Most of us know Cape plumbago as *Plumbago capensis,* but botanists now tell us that its correct name is *P. auriculata.* Under either name this tough shrub/vine is capable of producing a long show of the purest, most ethereal blue flowers in the hottest, sunniest situations. Strictly speaking, it is a sprawling, mounding shrub that can be used as a boundary planting, tall ground or bank cover, or large tub plant, but with a little support it can become a 12–foot vine.

Without natural climbing devices such as tendrils or twining branches it will need some tying up to trellis or arbor. It will also need some pinching of side shoots to encourage rapid lengthening of leading stems.

Light green, narrow leaves are 1 to 3–inches long, and look cool in hottest weather. Shoots are tipped by clusters of inch–wide flowers that greatly resemble those of garden or summer phlox *(Phlox suffruticosa).* Bloom continues from early spring through late autumn, sometimes almost the year around. It is important to buy plants in bloom, because seed–grown plants may have washed out, pale blue or whitish flowers. There is a pure white cultivated variety 'Alba', and a rich sky–blue cultivated variety named 'Royal Cape'.

Slow to start but quick to grow once well rooted, Cape plumbago can tolerate poor soil so long as drainage is reasonably good. Once established it needs little water and feeding. My plant grows on a hot, fiercely reflective south–facing white wall in poor clay soil. It receives no feeding and gets its water from winter rains and some summer seepage from an irrigated bank planting several feet away. Grooming consists of clipping off faded flower clusters and removing infrequent winter-blackened twigs.

DD

POLYGONUM AUBERTII
Polygonaceae
SILVER LACE VINE
Evergreen perennial

Should you want to cover an ugly shed or even a house, silver lace vine, *Polygonum aubertii,* may be the vine for you. It can grow 20 feet in one season, and once established takes little water. Like any other rampant plant, it benefits from frequent pruning to keep it in check. It can even be sheared like a hedge or cut to the ground.

Silver lace vine has handsome, heart shaped, shiny leaves, about 1 1/2 inches long, with foamy masses of cream-colored flowers which occur from spring through fall. The spent flowers have a silvery look, probably suggesting its common name.

This twining vine is so fast growing it requires wires or other support when first planted.

BC

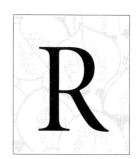

RHODOCHITON ATROSANGUINEUM
Scrophulariaceae
Tender perennial grown as an annual

This small-scale vine is a native of Mexico and frost tender. It has purple–black, tubular flowers with a pinkish red calyx, and will bloom all summer amid heart-shaped leaves. Choose a sheltered spot and protect it from frost. (Mine survived the winter, only to be eaten by a squirrel.)

Rhodochiton will bloom all year indoors in a bright light or in a greenhouse. After the flowers fall, the five-pointed calyces, looking like small umbrellas, remain on the vine for months.

Treated as an annual, it will bloom the first year from seed available from J. L. Hudson Seedsman. It is also available at Strybing Arboretum plant sales.

SA

RHODODENRON FRAGRANTISSIMUM
Ericaceae
Evergreen perennial

Rhododendrons are not easy to grow on the Peninsula; most are suited to the cool, wet climate and acid soils of the Northwest. Not, however, *Rhododendron fragrantissimum,* a loose, open, vinelike shrub of slow to moderate growth to 6 to 12 feet. There aren't any other rhododendrons easier to grow here.

Mine grows into a large viburnum for the required support. A trellis would do as well. It likes a light, acid soil best, but no special treatment is necessary. Although it gets regular water and has a cool root run, mine went through the drought years with little water and survived the 100-year freeze. It is never fertilized.

In fact, I forget about it until it blooms in spring with large, white trusses and its powerful fragrance perfumes the garden.

Plants to accompany it might include other rhododendrons, camellias, azaleas, viburnum and osmanthus.

MK

ROSA BANKSIAE
Rosaceae
LADY BANKS' ROSE
Evergreen perennial

Lady Banks' rose (*Rosa banksiae*) is one of many rose species that are true vines, and the only one commonly available in Bay Area nurseries. Its many virtues include evergreen foliage (partially deciduous in the very coldest sites in the coldest winters), absence of thorns, and a profusion of flowers. These, although small, are borne in showy clusters and literally cover the vines in early spring

Smooth green stems weave through any available support to a height of 20 feet or more, then drop trailing branches. Old plants are sometimes seen climbing to the tops of tall trees, which they turn into fountains of gold. They make superb chain–link fence disguises or screening for tennis–court backstops.

The commonest variety is 'Lutea', which has clusters of double, button–sized yellow flowers. Occasionally you can find the double white variety usually sold as 'Alba Plena' or white banksia; this has the added advantage of violet–scented perfume. The wild, single–flowered white and yellow forms are exceedingly rare.

Lady Banks' roses thrive in sun or light shade and endure ordinary well–drained garden soil. Once well established, they need little water in summer and only enough pruning to shape them or remove surplus growth. They are not subject to most rose diseases, although they sometimes suffer light damage from powdery mildew.

DD

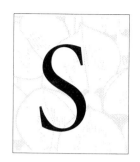

SEMELE ANDROGYNA
Liliaceae
CLIMBING BUTCHER'S BROOM
Evergreen perennial

Semele androgyna, climbing butcher's broom, is an outstanding foliage vine, even though it has no leaves to speak of. This apparent contradiction springs from the fact that apparent leaves are actually modified branches (cladophylls). True leaves are tiny scales along the main stem. In general appearance climbing butcher's broom resembles a climbing palm, the branch structure almost exactly counterfeiting the appearance of a feather-palm frond.

In early spring new stems emerge, looking precisely like asparagus spears (asparagus is a distant relative in the lily family). When these spears reach a height of 10 feet or so, you can be reasonably certain that they are not asparagus. They continue to grow, twining around any support they find, to a height of possibly 50 feet. On my plant they have reached perhaps 25 feet. Eventually primary branches break out from this stem at intervals of several inches; these grow to 18 to 20 inches in length and put out 20 to 24 leathery, deep green 3–inch by 1–inch cladophylls.

These giant, yet delicate, structures are evergreen and live for several years. In the second year tiny whitish flowers appear along the edges of the cladophylls. These will in a year after bloom produce bright red berries

Climbing butcher's broom is native to the Canary Islands, which should make it tender, but it has shown no signs of damage in 10 years. My specimen grows in the shade of a massive deodar, receives a monthly watering in the summer, and is fed once a year with acid plant food.

I have seen only three other examples, the one at Strybing (now removed); one at California Center in Los Angeles, where it was growing across a driveway under a building in almost total shade; and one growing unsupported at La Mortola in Italy, where it formed a sprawling mound 4 feet tall and 20 feet across.

DD

SENECIO CONFUSUS (PSEUDOGYNOXYS CHENOPODIOIDES)
Asteraceae (Compositae)
MEXICAN FLAME VINE
Evergreen perennial

Senecio confusus, the Mexican flame vine, has been given a new name of *Pseudogynoxys chenopodioides* but is still the same beautiful vine it has always been.

A member of Compositae, it is native to Colombia so is subject to frost damage. There seem to be two strains of this vine available from different sources. One has stems and toothed leaves that are tinged purple, the second with light green ovate foliage, some slightly toothed.

This vine should be planted in a warm protected spot and have excellent drainage as well as plenty of water.

It is a fairly rapid grower, 4 to 6 feet a year, ultimately to 15 to 20 feet. It is most effective if planted where it can weave up through another shrub where the clusters of bright orange daisies can be displayed. It would probably work as a ground cover on a sunny bank that is frost free. The tips of this vine will burn back with frost but it will recover quickly in the spring and summer. It will probably be killed by frosts of 20° or colder.

EC

SOLANDRA MAXIMA
Solanaceae
Cup-of-gold vine
Evergreen perennial

Solandra maxima, (sometimes confused with *S. guttata),* is an evergreen vine in Solanaceae from Mexico and Central America.

A strong–growing vine with rampant growth to 30 feet and large, 6 to 7–inch, elliptical leaves, the flowers are golden yellow, cup–shaped to 6 inches across with purple stripes or spots.

Solandra will cover large walls or fences, but must be tied or given support to hold it in place. Planted in a half barrel and trained under a sunny patio cover is an effective way to display the large flowers which bloom during the spring and occasionally throughout the summer.

This is a tough vine that will stand adverse conditions, but not heavy frosts.

There is a form with cream–variegated foliage that is most effective as the new growth develops. On the new leaves, the edges that, when mature will be a creamy yellow, are a soft violet color. The five or six small leaves at the tips of the new growth have this beautiful violet shading.

EC

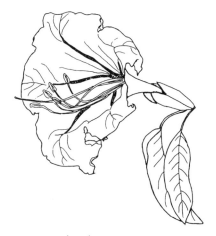

Solandra maxima

SOLANUM
Solanaceae
Potato vine
Semi-evergreen perennial

Similar to many others of this genus, *Solanum jasminoides* 'Album', the white potato vine, adapts to many conditions—it matters little whether it receives much or little water, good soil or heavy clay soil, full sun or part shade.

A fast–growing, evergreen perennial, it has dark green, oval leaves (some leaves on older parts of the plant are divided into leaflets). The small, white flower clusters appear almost continuously with purple berries in autumn. Frost tolerant to 26 degrees, it will lose its leaves in colder winters.

It is a carefree (relatively) vine to cover an ugly fence or extend a fence to exclude a view. Don't be afraid to cut it back or at least groom it once a year to avoid tangles.

Grasses and mullein at its feet would be a good combination.

Solanum crispum is a shrubby vine which also requires regular pruning to keep it within bounds. It needs a heavy–duty support and tying as it matures. A reward is its nine months of lavender-blue flower clusters.

Bearded and Dutch iris along with *Cerastium tomentosum* are complements.

Solanum wendlandii, Costa Rican nightshade or paradise flower, is a scrambler that uses the sharp hook–like spines along the canes to climb through shrubs or trees.

This vine has bright green stems and basal leaves that can be simple and entire while those closer to the terminal may be pinnate with several laterals. Most leaves will drop during the winter.

The 1 1/2–inch flowers are a beautiful blue to violet–blue in terminal clusters during the summer months.

Coming from the tropics, this solanum should be given a warm, sunny, protected spot. Since it can make 15 to 20 feet of growth, it must be given some sort of support to make the most of the flower display.

Costa Rican nightshade will probably be killed by frost below 25 degrees.

EC, LP, MG

SOLLYA HETEROPHYLLA (SOLLYA FUSIFORMIS)
Pittosporaceae
AUSTRALIAN BLUEBELL CREEPER
Evergreen perennial

Australian bluebell creeper, *Sollya heterophylla (S. fusiformis)*, is usually considered a ground cover shrub rather than a vine. Certainly most plants seen hereabouts are used as ground cover, although with support and training plants can grow 6 to 8 feet tall.

Its principal virtues are its delicate, fresh–looking bright green foliage and its summer–long production of clustered, drooping 1/2–inch bright blue flower bells. A white–flowered form is occasionally offered. Cylindrical blue 1/2–inch fruits follow, but are neither profuse nor conspicuous.

A weak twiner, it will need assistance in starting to climb, but it can make a light tracery on a trellis. It is attractive planted at the top of a wall and allowed to trail. Australian authorities suggest that plants grown from seed are variable, some being shrubby, others vinelike. If this is the case, shop for plants that promise to have the habit you want.

One unusual virtue of bluebell creeper is its ability to thrive under eucalyptus trees.

DD

STAUNTONIA HEXAPHYLLA
Lardizabalaceae
Evergreen perennial

Stauntonia hexaphylla is in Lardizabalaceae and is native to Korea and Japan. This evergreen twining vine can easily grow to 30 feet unless confined to a container as ours has been for at least 15 years. The dark green leathery leaves are stalked and divided into 3 to 7 leaflets.

It is monoecious with the male and female, white–tinged violet flowers born on separate racemes. The flowers make a good show for a short time during February and March.

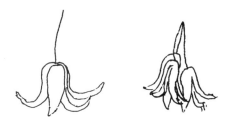

stauntonia hexaphylla female and male flowers

Our plant has set few fruit which may be the lack of the right pollinator or the result of being confined to a container. When mature the fruit is egg-shaped but larger, spotted purple to almost all purple when fully ripe. It is said to be edible but the many seeds are surrounded by very little mucilage so there is little to eat and quite tasteless.

Easily grown from seed, it is probably best grown as a container plant in part shade for those who want one of everything.

EC

STIGMAPHYLLON LITTORALE
Malpighiaceae
Orchid vine
Evergreen perennial

Stigmaphyllon littorale, a member of Malpighiaceae, is a hardier, larger cousin of *S. ciliatum*, the so-called orchid vine.

Although native to southern Brazil, this vine has survived Los Altos winters for a quarter century. A drop to 19 degrees killed the top, but the plant grew rapidly from the large, fleshy, dahlia-like roots in spring. The half-inch-thick stems grow astonishingly fast to 20 feet or more, with pairs of 5-inch oval leaves at intervals of 6 inches to 1 foot. In summer and early fall the 6-inch flower stalks appear from the leaf joints of the upper leaves. These stalks bear clusters of yellow, inch-wide flowers. Petals are round, but contracted at the base into a narrow claw. Uneven-sized petals have given the misleading name of orchid vine. Occasionally a flower cluster will sprout a secondary cluster from its center or its side.

This vine is not commonly grown and undoubtedly will be hard to find. It is primarily a curiosity for collectors, although its ropes of yellow flowers dangling from the top of a large avocado tree are certainly spectacular.

DD

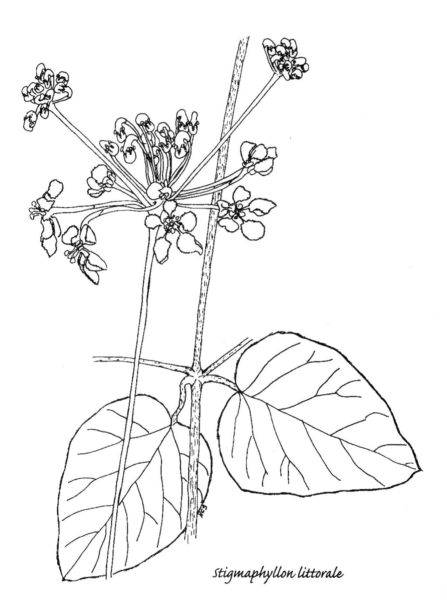

stigmaphyllon littorale

TECOMARIA CAPENSIS
Bignoniaceae
Cape honeysuckle
Evergreen perennial

Tecomaria capensis (Tecoma capensis), the Cape honeysuckle, is less vinelike than most of its bignonia cousins, but it can reach 20 feet or more if given a support and some tying-in. Bright green leaves are divided into many leaflets and the overall effect is delicate, although the plant is vigorous. Tight clusters of narrowly tubular bright orange-red, 2-inch flowers appear in fall and winter. The cultivated variety 'Aurea', with bright yellow flowers, may be preferred by those who like a milder color, or who merely like novelty.

Without training cape honeysuckle forms a tall, loose narrowish shrub. It needs cutting back often when young to encourage the bushy growth. Travelers familiar with New Zealand's North Island may recall miles of this plant used as a boundary hedge between fields. It is a native of South Africa, however.

Cape honeysuckle is highly tolerant of wind, heat, even seaside winds. It needs good drainage but needs little water once established. Use it to espalier along wall or fence. Hummingbirds love it.

DD, MB

THUNBERGIA
Acanthaceae
Perennial

Thunbergia alata, the black-eyed Susan vine, is a good choice for a colorful vine to quickly cover a fence, fill a hanging basket or drape down a retaining wall. It is by nature a sprawling plant, but it can easily be induced to twine up a support. The orange tubular flowers with their black throats make a fine display, but if a wall of bright orange seems a bit strident, there are also white, buff or yellow variants, with or without the black throats.

Thunbergia alata is easily grown from seed. Two sources are Burpee's and Thompson and Morgan. The seed will be in a mixture of colors of which the black–throated, orange combination will dominate, but it's fun to see what may pop up.

All thunbergias are tropical in origin and are not hardy much below freezing, but they will usually resprout from the roots. Because they seed about so freely, there is usually a crop of volunteers.

Good soil, water and plenty of heat are needed for best performance but a well–established plant can withstand a considerable period of drought because their tuberous roots store water.

There are two blue–flowered species of thunbergia that grow well in this area, Thunbergia grandiflora and Thunbergia laurifolia, both of which are magnificent vines growing to as much as 50 feet and bearing large blue flowers in profusion. The flowers of both are funnel–form, abruptly flaring at the mouth to a five–lobed corolla. The inside of the throat is creamy white to soft yellow.

Thunbergia laurifolia

Thunbergia grandiflora 'Augusta' flower

 Thunbergia grandiflora 'Augusta' is a selected form of the sky flower or blue sky flower, native to North India. This twining vine has dark green stems and elliptical toothed leaves. The 3–inch beautiful sky blue flowers occur in clusters of 5 to 7 at the leaf nodes on the new growth. It is a rampant grower with the greatest show of flowers during the summer months and with scattered bloom throughout the year. Ed Carman's plant has been grown in an unheated plastic house for several years where it is up to the 10–foot ridge and crawling along the ventilator controls. This perennial thunbergia would probably not be hardy in the garden unless grown in a very protected spot against the house. It might be worth trying in a container in a sunny patio that has a fiberglass roof.

 Thunbergia gregorii (T. gibsonii), clock vine, is from tropical Africa. This perennial vine can cover a 6–foot trellis in one season. The stems, leaves and flower bracts are all covered with fine hair. The 6–inch flower stems hold the purple-marked, 1 1/2–inch bract where the clear orange flower emerges from the bottom opening. The brilliant orange solitary flowers can cover the plant during the summer season.

 Ed Carman has grown his plant for several years in a container with a wire cone on top to keep the vine from getting out of hand. This thunbergia will freeze back in the winter, but has survived all but the 100-year freeze. It roots easily from cuttings but seldom sets seed.

 Rich soil and moisture are necessary, and they are slow to get started in the spring, needing warm soil temperatures. Naturally sprawling, they need a bit of coaxing to persuade them to climb which they eventually do after a long period of indecision by twining their leaves around a support like a clematis. They need to be shown which way is up by tying the early stems to the support.

EC, EG

TRACHELOSPERMUM
Apocynaceae
STAR JASMINE
Evergreen perennial

When the average Bay Area gardener speaks of jasmine he is probably thinking of star jasmine, *Trachelospermum jasminoides*. It is certainly far more widespread than any of the true jasmines, although more are used as ground cover than climbing vines. It is in the dogbane family (Apocynaceae), many members of which have milky sap and showy, fragrant flowers. (True jasmines are in the olive family.)

Given support, star jasmine will twine to 20 feet, possibly more. It is a slow starter, but when established makes considerable new growth each year and will profit from tip–pinching or thinning. The slender stems are closely set with glossy narrow dark green leaves to 3 inches long.

Flowers are star–shaped, white, about an inch wide, and carried in loose clusters at the ends of short side branches. The fragrance is sweet, with a hint of nutmeg, and is strongest on warm evenings. Flowering here usually occurs in June and July, but some blossoms may appear through the end of August. Dick Dunmire's plants clothe three posts on the front porch, from which they salute visitors with their fragrance. They receive the same irrigation and feeding as the camellias that front them; maintenance consists in cutting back long, straying late–summer growth and occasional trimming to preserve a respectable width.

There is a cultivated variety ('Variegata') with white variegation on the leaves.

Another star jasmine-type twiner, *Trachelospermum asiaticum* needs a trellis, where it creates a tropical effect with its evergreen leaves that have an occasional touch of red, and creamy yellow flowers scented differently from *Trachelospermum jasminoides*.

Trachelospermum asiaticum is excellent for a small to medium screen, 8 to 10 feet high. It is drought-tolerant once established and survived the 1990 freeze, but it requires afternoon shade or it will sunburn.

It has a tidy habit and there is no need to prune it.

DD, MK, EC

TROPAEOLUM
Tropaeolaceae
NASTURTIUM
Annual, perennial

The nasturtium most often seen *(Tropaeolum majus)* is an annual widely grown for color in difficult spots. Some climbing forms can be used for trellis or posts or to weave up other shrubbery.

Many elegant species of Tropaeolum are perennial and most form tubers. The one we have grown (probably a form of *T. tricolorum)* was given to us as seed with the name 'pink lady legs.' Several sprouted but only one survived to bloom after several years.

The delicate stems and five–parted leaves are a rich medium green. It climbs by the leaf stems twining around any handy support. As a support we use a dead leafless bamboo cane leaving all the side shoots attached as a trellis for this delicate vine.

The flowers are about one inch long, tubular, held vertically on slender 2-inch stems, with the opening down. The stem is attached near the slender pointed top so that the flower can move in the wind.

The flowers are a clear pink with a slight touch of green at the mouth of the tube. With a good imagination, the little pink flowers would look like tiny legs being held up at the ankles, hence the name 'pink ladies legs.'

Our plant has set seeds several times but none have ever germinated. It was about ten years before we were able to divide the tubers and then had only five!

These are cool weather plants with new growth sprouting in the fall and full bloom in the spring to early summer. It's a good plant for hummingbirds and a great delicacy for snails.

The summer heat sends them into dormancy for their rest period. A charming lacy vine, it is best grown as a container plant to be displayed while in flower and kept in the background while resting.

EC

VITIS CALIFORNICA
Vitaceae
CALIFORNIA GRAPE
Deciduous perennial

The native grape has insignificant fruit, but is grown instead for its gorgeous fall foliage. The cultivar 'Roger's Red' in October and November has leaf color in shades of burgundy, red, and orange in stippled, striated and other patterns. It is particularly lovely with light showing through. Others plants in the species are usually golden yellow.

A rampant grower, it needs a sturdy trellis or other support. It can make shade on a pergola or the main branch can be tied up to grow in a long line to emphasize a shape, such as an arch.

It can be pruned in December back to the main stem leaving two buds per spur. The following season, California grape can grow 15 feet after pruning. It prefers light shade.

In its native habitat, California grape grows near streams, and so requires regular water.

Edible small berries (grapes) appear in fall, but are best left for the birds or used for Thanksgiving decorations.

It is easy to propagate from cuttings or may be purchased from Yerba Buena Nursery, where a 30-foot specimen runs along the roofline of the office.

CC, MK

WISTERIA
Leguminoasae
Deciduous perennial

    Wisteria (*Wistaria*), a strong growing vine in Fabaceae
(Leguminosae), was named for an American professor, Caspar Wistar.
Native to China, Japan, and the southeastern U.S., there are 10 species of
this deciduous twining vine. Growing in the wild, these are found in
moist woodlands, streamside, and wherever there is a constant supply of
water. It is said that some of the most spectacular wisterias in Japan are
growing where the water is only two feet below the top of the soil.

    All wisterias have pinnate leaves and pea–shaped flowers in
racemes that measure from 8 inches to 4 feet in length. Flower colors vary
from purple to lilac to violet to blue shades, pink and white. There is
reputed to be a red form in Japan but it is probably not in the U.S. at this
time. Fruits are large beans with tough shells that if left on the vine will
explode and scatter seeds. When grown from seed, plants may take 10
years to flower and will then probably not be the same as the parent. In
the past these vines have been propagated mainly by grafting on seedling
wisteria, with a cleft or side graft. All growth from ground level of grafted
plants should be removed as it may be from the rootstock. Most wisteria
are now being grown from cuttings, so all growth will be the same.

    In the 1920's and 30's many named wisterias were imported
from Japan by Domoto Nursery in Hayward, and W.B. Clarke Nursery in
San Jose. When those nurseries closed, most of the named wisterias were
lost and only now are again becoming available. The most widely planted
wisterias are the Japanese and Chinese, while the U.S. natives are seldom
seen. The direction that the wisterias twine and the number of leaflets are
two features that help to identify the type. *Wisteria floribunda* (Japanese
wisteria) twines in a clockwise direction and the leaves have 13 to 19
leaflets. The flower clusters vary from 18 inches to more than four feet
and the flowers open from the base to the apex.

Many cultivars have been named in Japan, some for the towns or the area where they were first grown. The most outstanding of these is *W.floribunda* 'Macrobotrys' which has 4-foot racemes of purple-blue flowers. *W. floribunda* 'Violacea Plena' has double violet-blue flowers, the darkest now available. A fine specimen can be seen at Filoli Gardens.

W.floribunda 'Alba' is one of the best white forms of the Japanese wisterias with racemes about two feet long and blooms in great profusion. *W.f.* 'Rosea' has pale pink to rosy pink flowers in rather open trusses. *W.f.* 'Issai' is possibly a hybrid, with lilac-blue flowers in 15-inch trusses. It blooms as a young plant and early in the season.

Wisteria sinensis (Chinese wisteria) has leaves with 9 to 13 leaflets. It twines counter-clockwise. The 8 to 15-inch racemes appear with the leaves and colors range from mauve to lilac to white and purple. When in bloom, some plants of this species are a solid mass of color. *W.sinensis* 'Caroline' is a hybrid that was selected at UCLA in the 60's. It is a dependable bloomer in areas that have warm winters. Mauve flowers appear in spring and early summer.

Wisteria venusta (*W. brachybotrys*) has has long been cultivated in Japan, where it is rare in the wild. The white flowers are held somewhat upright and the florets are largest of all wisteria and very fragrant. It seldom sets seed.

Wisteria frutescens is a native of the southeastern U.S. It is a rather slow grower with 5 to 17 leaflets. The pale purple to lilac flowers are in racemes, about 8 inches long. There are many other wisterias listed but in many cases the same plant has been given several names.

Wisterias are extremely strong growing vines and must be grown on a sturdy structure. The most important element in early training is to keep them from twining around any support as they can crush any timber smaller than 4 inches by 4 inches. Training should begin with planting while the new growth is still pliable. If used to cover a fence or wall, staples or eyes of some sort should be attached to the structure so that plastic ties can be used to hold the vine in place. The object is to train the canes that will become the main framework of the wisteria and will be kept in place for the life of the plant. The side shoots from the main cordon will become the flowering spurs. The growth from the spurs should be pruned each year after the vines are fully dormant.

If grown on an overhead arbor, wisterias should be trained along the top of supports that are spaced so that pruning can be done from below.

Wisteria sinensis

Contributors

Fran Adams	FA
Sherry Austin	SA
Barbara Barlow	BB
Louise Blakey	LB
Marjorie Branagh	MB
Rosamond Bray	RB
Ed Carman	EC
Barrie Coate	BC
Mabel Crittenden	MC
Carolyn Curtis	CC
Dick Dunmire	DD
Jean Fowkes	JF
Maggie Gage	MG
Elizabeth Garbett	EG
Doug Heimforth	DH
Mary Kaye	MK
C. Todd Kennedy	CTK
Elaine Levine	EL
Nancy McClenny	NM
Carol Moholt	CM
David and Dorothy Rodal	DR
Judy Wong	JW
Barbara Worl	BW

Sources

Nurseries

Carman's Nursery, 16201 E. Mozart Ave., Los Gatos, CA 95032. Phone: (408) 356-0119

ForestFarm. 990 Tetherow Road, Williams, OR 97544–9599. Phone: (503) 846-7269

Wayside Gardens, 1 Garden Lane, Hodges, SC 29695-0001. Phone: (800) 845-1124

Western Hills, 16250 Coleman Valley Road, Occidental, CA 95465. Phone: (707) 874-3731

Yerba Buena Nursery, 19500 Skyline Blvd., Woodside, CA 94062. Phone (415) 851-1668

Seed companies

W. Atlee Burpee & Co., Warminster, PA 18974. Phone: (800) 888-1447

Nichols Garden Nursery, 1190 N. Pacific Highway, Albany, OR 97321-4580. Phone: (541) 928-9280

J. L. Hudson Seedsman, P. O. Box 1058, Redwood City, CA 94064

Geo. W. Park Seed Co., Inc., Cokesbury Road, Greenwood, SC 26647-0001. Phone: (864) 223-7333

Redwood City Seed Company, P.O. Box 361, Redwood City, CA 94064. Phone: (415) 325-SEED

Thompson & Morgan, Inc., P. O. Box 1308, Jackson, NJ 08527-0308. Phone: (800) 274-7333

Plant sales

California Native Plant Society, Santa Clara Valley Chapter, c/o Peninsula Conservation Center, 3921 E. Bayshore Rd., Palo Alto, CA 94303. Phone: (415) 962-9876

Strybing Arboretum, Ninth Ave. at Lincoln Way, San Francisco, 94122. Phone: (415) 661-1316

Western Horticultural Society, P. O. Box 60507, Palo Alto, CA 94306. Phone: (408) 356-0119

Quick Reference Table

Botanical Name	Flower Color	Growth Rate	Exposure	Water Use
Abutilon megapotamicum	red/yellow	rapid	part shade	moderate
Actinidia deliciosa	creamy	rapid	full sun	moderate
Akebia quinata	white, purple	rapid	shade, sun/ part shade	moderate
Ampelopsis	white	moderate	any	moderate
Aristolochia californica	cream	slow to start	part shade	ample
Asarina scandens	lavender	rapid	sun	moderate
Asparagus falcatus	white	rapid	sun	moderate
Billardiera longiflora	pale green	rapid	sun/part shade	moderate
Bougainvillea glabra	all colors	moderate	sun	low
Calystegia macrostegia	pink	rapid	sun	low
Canarina canariensis	apricot pink	rapid	part shade	moderate
Celastrus scandens	greenish	rapid	sun	moderate
Cissus striatus	white	moderate	sun, shade	moderate
Clematis	many	moderate	sun	high
Clematis lasiantha	white	rapid	sun	low
Clematis ligusticifolia	white	rapid	sun	low
Clytostoma callistegioides	lavender	rapid	sun/part shade	moderate
Cobaea scandens	purple	rapid	sun	moderate
Distictis buccinatoria	red	rapid	sun	moderate
Dolichos lablab	purple	rapid	sun	moderate
Eccremocarpus scaber	orange	rapid	sun	moderate

Quick Reference Table (cont.)				
Botanical Name	**Flower Color**	**Growth Rate**	**Expose**	**Water Use**
Fatshedera	greenish-yellow	moderate	part shade	moderate
Ficus Pumila	insignificant	slow to start, rapid later	shade, part shade	moderate
Gelsemium sempervirens	yellow	moderate	sun	moderate
Hardenbergia	purple	moderate	sun	moderate
Hedera	greenish	slow	part to full shade	low
Hibbertia scandens	yellow	rapid	sun	moderate
Hoya carnosa	white	slow	shade	moderate
Humulus lupulus	green	rapid	sun	moderate
Hydrangea seemannii	white	slow	part to full shade	moderate
Ipomoea nil	all but yellow	rapid	sun	low
Ipomoea alba	white	rapid	sun	low
Ipomoea lobata	red	rapid	sun	moderate
Ipomoea x sloteri	blue	rapid	sun	low
Jasminum grandiflorum	white	rapid	sun	moderate
Jasminum nitidum	white	moderate	sun	moderate
Jasminum polyanthum	white	moderate	sun	moderate
Lapageria rosea	pink	moderate	part shade	moderate
Lonicera periclymenum	yellow plus pink	rapid	sun	moderate
L. japonica 'Aureoreticulat'	cream	moderate	sun to part shade	moderate

Quick Reference Table (cont.)

Botanical Name	Flower Color	Growth Rate	Expose	Water Use
Lycianthes rantonnei	purple	moderate	sun	low
Macfadyena unguis-cati	yellow	rapid	sun	low
Mandevilla laxa	white	moderate	sun	moderate
Metrosiderouscarmineus	red	slow	sun	moderate
Momordica charantia	yellow	rapid	sun	moderate
Muehlenbeckia complexa	insig.	moderate	sun to part shade	low
Pandorea	white, pink, yellow	rapid	sun to part shade	moderate
Parthenocissus henryana	insig.	moderate	shade to part shade	moderate
P. quinquefolia	insig.	rapid	any	moderate
P. tricuspidata	insig.	rapid	any	moderate
Passiflora alato-caerula	white &, blue	rapid	sun	moderate
P. 'Lavender Lady'	lavender	rapid	sun	moderate
Phaseolus coccineus	red	rapid	sun	moderate
Philadelphus mexicanus	cream	rapid	sun	moderate
Plumbago auriculata	blue	moderate	sun	low
Polygonum aubertii	crmy. white	rapid	sun	moderate
Rhodochiton atrosanguineum	red-purple	moderate	part shade	moderate
Rhododendron fragrantissimum	white	slow	shade	high
Rosa banksiae	yellow or white	rapid	sun	moderate

Quick Reference Table (cont.)

Botanical Name	Color	Growth Rate	Expose	Water Use
Semele androgyne	insignificant	moderate	sun to part shade	low
Senecio confusus	orange-red	moderate	sun to part shade	high
Solandra maxima	yellow	rapid	sun	moderate
Solanum crispum	lilac-blue	rapid	sun	moderate
Solanum jasminoides	white	rapid	sun	moderate
Solanum wendlandii	lilac-blue	rapid	sun	moderate
Sollya heterophylla	blue	moderate	sun	moderate to low
Stauntonia hexaphylla	white/purple	moderate	shade	high
Stigmaphyllon littorale	yellow	rapid	part shade	high
Tecomaria capensis	orange-red	rapid	sun	low
Thunbergia alata	orange	rapid	sun to part shade	low
T. grandiflora 'Augusta'	blue	moderate	sun	moderate
T. gregorii (gibonsii)	orange	moderate	sun	moderate
Trachelospermum jasminoides	white	moderate	sun	moderate
T. jasminoides 'Variegata'	white	slow	sun to part shade	moderate
Tropaelum tricolorum	pink	moderate	part shade	moderate
Vius californica	insig.	rapid	sun	moderate to low
Wisteria	lavender, white	rapid	sun to part shade	moderate to low

Index

K

Kiwi vine *1*

Lablab purpureus 24
Lady Banks' rose *60*
Lapageria rosea 43
   L. rosea 'White Cloud' 43
Lonicera 45
   L. periclymenum 'Serotina' 45
   L. japonica 'Aureoreticulata' 45
   L. periclymenum 'Belgica' 45
Lycianthes rantonnetii 46
   L. rantonnetii 'Royal Robe' 46

M

Mandevilla laxa 48
Mandevilla suaveolens 48
Mattress vine *50*
Metrosideros carmina 48
Mexican flame vine *62*
Mina lobata 39
Mock orange, evergreen *56*
Momordica charantia 49
Muehlenbeckia complexa 50

N

Nasturtium *73*

O

Orchid vine *66*

P

Pandorea 51
   P. jasminoides 'Alba' 51
   P. jasminoides 'Lady D' 51
   P. jasminoides 'Rosea' 51
   P. pandorana 51
Paradise flower *64*
Paraguay nightshade *46*
Parthenocissus 52
   P. tricuspidata 'Veitchii' 53
Parthenocissus quinquefolia 52

Parthenocissus tricuspidata 52
Passiflora 53–55
   P. 'Lavender Lady' 55
   Passiflora alata-caerulea 54
   Passiflora edulis 53
   Passiflora pfordtii 54
Passion vine *53*
Phaedranthus buccinatorium 23
Phaseolus coccinea 56
Philadelphus mexicanus 56
Pipevine *6*
Plumbago auriculata 57
   P. auriculata 'Alba' 57
Plumbago capensis 57
Polygonum aubertii 58
Potato vine *64*
Pseudogynoxys chenopodioides 62

Q

Quamoclit x sloteri 38

R

Rhododenron x fragrantissimum 59
Rosa banksiae 60
   R. banksiae 'Alba Plena' 60
   R. banksiae 'Lutea' 60

S

Scarlet runner bean *56*
Semele androgyna 61
Senecio confusus 62
Sickle thorn asparagus *9*
Silver lace vine *58*
Silver-veined creeper *53*
Solandra maxima 63
Solanum 64
Solanum crispum 64
Solanum jasminoides
   S. jasminoides 'Album' 64
Solanum rantonnetii 46
Solanum wendlandii 64
Sollya fusiformis 65
Sollya heterophylla 65